# LAS MUJERES

Copymat opens @
730 Mon

## Project Staff

SUE DAVIDSON, *Editor*

MERLE FROSCHL, *Field-Testing Coordinator*

FLORENCE HOWE, *Director*

ELIZABETH PHILLIPS, *Editor*

SUSAN TROWBRIDGE, *Design and Production Director*

ALEXANDRA WEINBAUM, *Teaching Guide Editor*

# LAS MUJERES

## Conversations from a Hispanic Community

**Nan Elsasser**
**Kyle MacKenzie**
**Yvonne Tixier y Vigil**

**Photographs by Susan Trowbridge**

**The Feminist Press**
OLD WESTBURY, NEW YORK

**The McGraw-Hill Book Company**
NEW YORK, ST. LOUIS, SAN FRANCISCO

**Cover Photograph.** Left to right: Louisa Vigil, Ida Gutiérrez, Debbie Martínez.

**Frontispiece Photograph.** Kyle MacKenzie tapes a conversation with a Hispanic student attending the University of New Mexico.

**Library of Congress Cataloging in Publication Data**

Elsasser, Nan, 1945–
    Las mujeres: conversations from a Hispanic community.

    (Women's lives / women's work)
    Consists chiefly of interviews (some in both English and Spanish)
    Includes bibliographic references and index.
    1. Hispanic American women—New Mexico—Biography. 2. Hispanic American women—New Mexico—Social conditions. 3. New Mexico—Biography. I. MacKenzie, Kyle, joint author. II. Tixier y Vigil, Yvonne, joint author. III. Title. IV. Series.
F805.S75E45    305.4'8    80–20200
ISBN 0–912670–84–3 (Feminist Press)
ISBN 0–912670–70–3 pbk. (Feminist Press)
ISBN 0–07–020445–5 pbk. (McGraw-Hill)

The findings and conclusions of this volume do not necessarily represent the views of the National Endowment for the Humanities.

According to agreement between the authors and the women interviewed by them, fifty per cent of authors' royalties for *Las Mujeres* will be used to establish a scholarship fund for Hispanas.

# Table of Contents

# Publisher's Acknowledgments

Early in 1973, Mariam Chamberlain and Terry Saario of the Ford Foundation spent one day visiting The Feminist Press on the campus of the State University of New York, College at Old Westbury, They heard staff members describe the early history of The Feminist Press and its goal—to change the sexist education of girls and boys, women and men, through publishing and other projects. They also heard about those books and projects then in progress; they felt our sense of frustration about how little we were able to do directly for the classroom teacher. Advising us about funding, Terry Saario was provocative. "You need to think of yourselves," she said, "in the manner of language labs, testing and developing new texts for students and new instructional materials for teachers." Our "language" was feminism, our intent to provide alternatives to the sexist texts used in schools. The conception was, in fact, precisely the one on which the Press had been founded.

Out of that 1973 meeting came the idea for the *Women's Lives / Women's Work* project. This project, which would not officially begin for more than two years, has allowed us to extend the original concept of The Feminist Press to a broader audience.

We spent the years from 1973 to 1975 assessing the needs for a publication project, writing a major funding proposal, steering it through two foundations, negotiating with the Webster Division of McGraw-Hill, our co-publisher. We could not have begun this process without the advice and encouragement of Marilyn Levy of the Rockefeller Family Fund, from which we received a planning grant in 1973. For one year, Phyllis Arlow, Marj Britt, Merle Froschl, and Florence Howe surveyed the needs of teachers for books about women, reviewed the sexist bias of widely used history and literature texts, and interviewed editorial staffs of major educational publishers about their intentions to publish material on women. The research accumulated provided a strong case for the grant proposal first submitted to the Ford Foundation in the summer of 1974.

During the winter of 1974–75, Merle Froschl, Forence Howe, Corrine Lucido, and attorney Janice Goodman (for The Feminist Press) negotiated a co-publishing contract with McGraw-Hill. We could not have proceeded without the strong interest of John Rothermich of McGraw-Hill's Webster Division. Our co-publishing agreement gives control over editorial content and design to The Feminist Press; McGraw-Hill is responsible for distribution of the series to the high school audience, while The Feminist Press is responsible for distribution to colleges, bookstores, libraries, and the general public.

In the summer of 1975, the final proposal—to produce for co-publication a series of twelve supplementary books and their accompanying teaching guides—was funded by the Ford Foundation and the Carnegie Corporation. Project officers Terry Saario and Vivien Stewart were supportive and helpful throughout the life of the project. In 1978, The Feminist Press received funds from the National Endowment for the Humanities to help complete the project. Additional funds also were received from the Edward W. Hazen Foundation and from the Rockefeller Family Fund.

Once initial funding was obtained, The Feminist Press began its search for additional staff to work on the project. The small nucleus of existing staff working on the project was expanded as The Feminist Press hired new employees. The *Women's Lives / Women's Work* project staff ultimately included six people who remained for the duration of the project: Sue Davidson, Merle Froschl, Florence Howe, Elizabeth Phillips, Susan Trowbridge, and Alexandra Weinbaum. Mary Mulrooney, a member of the project staff through 1979, thereafter continued her work as a free-lance production associate for the duration of the project. We also wish to acknowledge the contributions of Dora Janeway Odarenko and Michele Russell, who were on staff through 1977; and Shirley Frank, a Feminist Press staff member who was a member of the project staff through 1979. Helen Schrader participated on the project during its first year, and kept financial records and wrote financial reports for the duration of the project.

The *Women's Lives / Women's Work* project staff adopted the methods of work and the decision-making structure developed by The Feminist Press staff as a whole. As a Press "work committee," the project met weekly to make decisions, review progress, discuss problems. The project staff refined the editorial direction of the project, conceptualized and devised guidelines for the books and teaching guides, and identified prospective authors. When proposals came in, the project staff read and evaluated the submissions and made decisions regarding them. Similarly, when manuscripts arrived, the project staff read and commented on them. Project staff members took turns drafting memoranda, reports, and other documents. And the design of the series grew out of the discussions and the ideas generated at the project meetings. The books, teaching guides, and other informational materials had the advantage, at significant stages of development, of the committee's collective direction.

Throughout the life of the project, The Feminist Press itself continued to function and grow. Individuals on staff who were not part of the *Women's Lives / Women's Work* project provided support and advice to the project: Jeanne Bracken, Brenda Carter, Shirley Frank, Brett Harvey, Frances Kelley, Carol Levin, Kam Murrin, Karen Raphael, Helen Schrader, Nancy Shea, Nivia Shearer, Anita Steinberg, Sharon Wigutoff, and Sophie Zimmerman.

The process of evaluation by teachers and students before final publication was as important as the process for developing ideas into books. To this end, we produced testing editions of the books. Field-testing networks were set up throughout the United States in a variety of schools—public, private, inner-city, small town, suburban, and rural— to reach as diverse a student population as possible. We field tested in the following cities, regions, and states: Boston, Massachusetts; Tampa, Florida; Greensboro, North Carolina; Tucson, Arizona; Los Angeles, California; Eugene, Oregon; Seattle, Washington; Shawnee Mission, Kansas; Martha's Vineyard, Massachusetts; New York City; Long Island; New Jersey; Rhode Island; Michigan; Minnesota. We also had an extensive network of educators—350 teachers across the country—who reviewed the books in the series, often using sections of books in classrooms. From teachers' and students' comments, questionnaires, and discussions, we gained valuable information both for revising the books and for developing the teaching guides.

Although there is no easy way to acknowledge the devotion and enthusiasm of hundreds of teachers who willingly volunteered their time and energies, we would like to thank the following teachers— and their students—with whom we worked directly in the testing of *Las Mujeres: Conversations from a Hispanic Community.* In Arizona, Sherry O'Donnell, Acting Chairperson of the Women's Studies Committee, the University of Arizona, and Betty Newlon, Professor of Education, the University of Arizona—with the assistance of Kay Kavanaugh—helped to contact the following teachers in the Tucson area: Mary Lynn Hamilton, Mari Helen High, Dorothy Livieratos, Beverly Middleton-Johnson, Kristin Wallace. We also wish to acknowledge Myra Dinnerstein, Chairperson of the Women's Studies Committee, for her help in the development of the Tucson network. In California, Lilyan Frank in the Department of English at the University of Southern California helped to contact teachers in the Los Angeles area: Sharon Geltner, Helen Kelly, Rhonda Nalisnik, Marion Walker, Ira West. In Eugene, Oregon, Bev Melugin, Instructional Materials Analyst, and Anne Stewart, Coordinator of Women's Programs, Lane Community College, helped to contact the following teachers: Kate Barry, Yvonne Fasold, Orris L. Goode, Ann Monro, Ronalee Ramsay, Harriet Wilson. In Seattle, Washington, Audra Adelberger of Feminists Northwest, and Edith Ruby, Sex Balance Curriculum Consultant to the Seattle public schools, helped to contact the following teachers: Roxie Day, Shirley Dunphy, Sara Kaplan, Suzanna Kline, Nancy Mason, Laurel Ann Pickett. We also wish to acknowledge the participation of Eleanor Bilimoria, Larae Glennon, Sharon Greene, Cynthia Lambarth, Ruth Pelz, and Gisela E. Taber.

We are grateful to Joan Augerot of the Seattle Public Schools multiethnic curriculum for many useful suggestions made in the testing stage of *Las Mujeres,* as well as for her careful reading of the galley proofs. As a New Mexican Hispana, she was an invaluable consultant throughout. We would also like to thank Kaye Briegel, California State University at Long Beach, for supplying historical sources and for her helpful commentary on the final draft of the manuscript.

Three times during the life of the *Women's Lives / Women's Work* project, an Advisory Board composed of feminist educators and scholars met for a full day to discuss the books and teaching guides. The valuable criticisms and suggestions of the following people who participated in these meetings were essential to the project: Mildred Alpern, Rosalynn Baxandall, Peggy Brick, Ellen Cantarow, Elizabeth Ewen, Barbara Gates, Clarisse Gillcrist, Elaine Hedges, Nancy Hoffman, Susan Klaw, Alice Kessler-Harris, Roberta Kronberger, Merle Levine, Eleanor Newirth, Judith Oksner, Naomi Rosenthal, Judith Schwartz, Judy Scott, Carroll Smith-Rosenberg, Adria Steinberg, Barbara Sussman, Amy Swerdlow. We also want to express our gratitude to Shirley McCune and Nida Thomas, who acted in a general advisory capacity and made many useful suggestions; and to Kathryn Girard and Kathy Salisbury, who helped to develop the teacher and student field-testing questionnaires.

We are indebted to Susan Trowbridge, who, covering many miles in New Mexico and getting acquainted with her subjects in a brief span of time, supplied the excellent photographs which enrich this book.

Other people whom we wish to thank are Charles Carmony, who prepared the index; Miriam Hurewitz, who copyedited the manuscript; Ruth Adam for the photo retouching; Randi Book of McGraw-Hill for administrative assistance; and Emerson W. Madairy of Monotype Composition Company for technical assistance.

The work of the many people mentioned in these acknowledgments has been invaluable to us. We would also like to thank all of you who read this book—because you helped to create the demand that made the *Women's Lives / Women's Work* project possible.

THE FEMINIST PRESS

# Authors' Acknowledgments

Like history, this book was made by many people whose names do not appear on the title page or in the table of contents. We would like to express our gratitude to some of those who helped us in the creation of *Las Mujeres*.

Our first thanks go to the women, children, and men who made possible the text and the photographic illustrations, through sharing their time, their thoughts, and their stories: Graham Allison, Guy Allison, Linda Armas, María Avila, Cathy Baca, José Delgado Baca, María Baca, Terry Flores Baca, Gilda Baeza, Viola Barela, Kathy Brooks, Juan Candelaria, Katie Candelaria, Tony Candelaria, Santos Carrillo, Gloria Gutiérrez Castillo, Teresa Cuarón, Bernadette Dávalos, Petra Silva Dávalos, Gloria de Tevis, Beverly Flores, Teresa Flores, Eloisa Gallegos, Irene García, Emma Gonzales, Dolores Griego, Dora Gutiérrez, Ida Gutiérrez, Ida P. Gutiérrez, Lorraine Gutiérrez, Nettie Gutiérrez, Jonella Haynes, Ruby Hatfield, Mildred Hernández, Petra Jaramillo, Bernie López, Patricia Luna, Ruby Luna, DeeDee Márquez, Teresa Márquez, Debbie Martínez, Edwina Martínez, Liz Martínez, Linda Mendez, Margie Mendez, Emma Metzger, Donna Montano, Juanita Montano, Barbara Montoya, Jennie Montoya, Marcos Montoya, Stella Montoya, Tanya Montoya, Donaldo Orioste, Johnina Ortega, Feliz Ortega, Josephine Ortiz, Leroy Ortiz, Andreita Padilla, Beverly Sánchez Padilla, Bernadette Padilla, Delilah Padilla, Lina Padilla, Lucy Padilla, Rafael Padilla, Susana Padilla, Frances Parrish, Ellen Press, Helen Quintana, Carol Reider, Alexis Rindone, Pier Rindone, Pauline Rindone, Rene Rindone, Delfina Romo, Elsie Sánchez, James Sánchez, Jennie Sánchez, Lynn Sánchez, Judy Sandoval, Paula Sandoval, Jacinta Santiago, Jacqueline Santiago, Mara Santiago, Nina Santiago, Rita Santiago, Mary Jo Sarason, Juanita Sedillo, Romaine Serna, M. Perlinda Sheldon, Mary Sigula, Veronica Suárez, Mara Taub, Adelita Tijerina, Florence Tixier, Frank Turrietta, JoAnn Turrietta, Joseph Turrietta, Josephine Turrietta, Lulu Turrietta, Susie Turrietta, Valentina Valdez, Vera Valdez, Flora Vásquez, Louisa Vigil.

We would also like to thank the following people for reading and giving valuable comments on the manuscript in its various drafts, and for suggesting possible publishers: Rudy Anaya, Helen Bannan, Kathy Brooks, Pat D'Andrea, Gloria de Tevis, Susan de Witt, Ruth Elsasser, Lucien Ferster, Nancy Gage, Margaret García, Samuel B. Girgus, Alice H. MacKenzie, Ossian H. MacKenzie, Ann Nihlen, Leroy Ortiz,

Pauline Rindone, Stan Steiner, Vera John Steiner, Mara Taub, Albert Vogel, Marta Weigle.

We are grateful to those who helped with interpreting and translating various portions of the manuscript: Haldane Chase, María del Rosario García, Leroy Ortiz, Candy Martínez.

We would like to recognize the valuable assistance of Roberta Benecke and Nancy Gage, who typed and retyped *Las Mujeres*— always under less than ideal conditions. We would also like to recognize Susan Conway and Robert Levy's generous donation of legal expertise.

We would like to thank Sue Davidson, our Feminist Press editor, for her guidance in the organization and development of the manuscript, for her participation in identifying and clarifying its basic themes, and for her careful editing of each successive draft.

And finally, there are writers whose works have sustained and encouraged us: Garbriel García Márquez, Studs Terkel, and Alice Walker.

NAN ELSASSER
KYLE MACKENZIE
YVONNE TIXIER Y VIGIL

# Preface

*Las Mujeres* is a collection of life stories told to us by Hispanic women of New Mexico—women who call themselves Chicanas, women who call themselves Spanish, women who call themselves Spanish-American, Mexican-American, and Mexican—*mujeres* speaking together to create an oral history of Hispanas' experiences in the Southwest.*

The women speaking in this book are great-grandmothers and great-granddaughters. They are city women and country women. They are farmers, politicians, factory workers, teachers, artists, and housemaids. They have described their work and their lives because they want to help make a written record of a culture and a heritage which, while omitted from written history, has been passed on orally, like much of women's culture, from mother to daughter, from grandmother to grandchild.

**The Hispanic Women of New Mexico.** Who are the Hispanic women of New Mexico? Historically, this question has several answers, one of them beginning 400 years ago when Spanish and Mexican colonists emigrated north from Mexico to settle in the upper Rio Grande valley. Some of these colonists were direct descendants of the Spanish *conquistadores*; some were descended from unions of the Spanish with Indian peoples of Mexico. Further racial and cultural mixing occurred in New Mexico through the unions of the colonists with Indian people who had settled in the region thousands of years earlier.

Mexico achieved final independence from Spain in 1821; however, almost the entire northern half of Mexico was annexed by the United States as the outcome of its war with Mexico (1846–1848). The territory taken over in that war is the present day southwestern United States that includes New Mexico. Emigration from Mexico to the southwest increased after the Mexican Revolution (1910), and continues today. Thus, some Hispanas trace their New Mexican origins back hundreds of years, while others are more recent arrivals. The heritage of New

---

* Many of the older women, emphasizing their Spanish heritage, referred to themselves as Spanish. Others spoke of "coming from Mexico," or called themselves Mexican, as did some of the younger generations. Also, the younger women we interviewed often called themselves Chicana, a term reflecting their political identification, their Indian ancestry, and pride in their southwestern heritage. In writing of these women collectively, we have referred to them as Hispanic, a term referring broadly to Spanish-speaking people.

Mexican Hispanas as a group includes Spanish, Indian, and Mexican elements.*

**How This Book Was Written.** The interviews for *Las Mujeres* were conducted and transcribed by Yvonne Tixier y Vigil and Nan Elsasser. Several interviews were conducted totally or partially in Spanish. These Spanish interviews were transcribed and translated by Nan Elsasser, who preserved the regional characteristics of the language in her transcription. The *Las Mujeres* project was coordinated by Kyle MacKenzie, who also served as principal editor. All three collaborated closely in collecting interviews and writing the volume's Preface, Prologue, and section introductions.

Most of the women we interviewed came from Albuquerque and the surrounding semirural areas. Several of the younger women were friends of ours, students we had taught at the University of Albuquerque and women we had gone to school with at the University of New Mexico (UNM). We met many of the older women at the Senior Citizens' Center in Los Padillas, a small town about twenty minutes south of Albuquerque. We also conducted interviews in the northern mountain towns of New Mexico and in the southern part of the state. In all, we interviewed ninety-three women, ranging in age from seventeen to eighty-seven and covering a span of roughly four generations.

We began collecting these interviews in the autumn of 1975. Our methods were informal, as were the settings and the circumstances in which the interviews took place. There were afternoons when, in the

* Rosura Sánchez and Rosa Martínez Cruz, eds., *Essays on La Mujer* (Anthology No. 1, Chicano Studies Center Publications, University of California at Los Angeles); Martha P. Cotera, *Diosa y Hembra: The History and Heritage of Chicanas in the U.S.* (Austin, Texas: Information Systems Development, 1976); Rodolfo Acuña, *Occupied America: The Chicano's Struggle Toward Liberation* (San Francisco: Canfield Press, 1972); Carey McWilliams, *North from Mexico: The Spanish-Speaking People in the United States* (New York: Greenwood Press, 1968); Julian Samora and Patricia Vandel Simon, *A History of the Mexican-American People* (Notre Dame, Ind.: University of Notre Dame Press, 1977); and Matt Meier and Feliciano Rivera, *The Chicanos: A History of Mexican Americans* (New York: Hill & Wang, 1972), all describe the history and heritage of people of Mexican descent in the United States. Those in New Mexico are discussed in Nancie González, *The Spanish-Americans of New Mexico: A Heritage of Pride* (Albuquerque: University of New Mexico Press, 1967); and Frances Leon Swadesh, *Los Primeros Pobladores: Hispanic Americans on the Ute Frontier* (Notre Dame, Ind.: University of Notre Dame Press, 1974).

space of three hours, we listened to a whole family of mothers, cousins, and daughters. There were four months stretching over a spring and summer in which we visited with women at the Senior Citizens' Center in Los Padillas, learning how to make *sopa* (bread pudding)* and how to string *chiles*, waiting while these women decided whether they would talk about their lives on tape. Gradually, the group of speakers grew by word of mouth, as one woman after another asked her friends and relatives to talk. With these life stories came poems and recipes, invitations to dinner and *fiestas*, and friendships with women we would otherwise never have met.

Once we had taped and transcribed the interviews, we edited them and divided them roughly into four age groups. To give readers an idea of the basic form of the original interviews, we retained the questions and answers in the first interview in this book, with Louisa Vigil. Other interviews were edited into monologue form.

Because we had collected many more interviews than we could include between the covers of one book, we selected a group of them which reflect the common cultural concerns and customs in each generation, while also demonstrating the differing personal situations, attitudes, and ideas of the women.

After this selection had been made, we returned the edited interviews to each speaker for her approval. Upon request, we have changed the names of some of the women.† However, the stories they tell are wholly their own.

As the stories were assembled in their final order, it became possible to identify certain pervasive major themes. A respect for the people, the ideas, and the customs of the past, a strong concern with woman's place in the family, a desire for improved educational opportunities, a determination to work for social change, weave in and out of the conversations of Hispanic grandmothers, mothers, daughters, and granddaughters. While all of these themes are present to some degree in every section, in certain generations a particular theme achieves distinct importance. When we selected Spanish proverbs as the basis for section titles, these themes were our guides.‡

* *Sopa* is also the common Spanish word for soup. See Glossary.

† The following names used in the text are fictitious: Susana Archuleta, Experanza Salcido, Kathy Alarid, Margaret Torres, and Ana Germini.

‡ Our main source was *Dichos: Proverbs and Sayings from the Spanish*, collected and translated by Charles Aranda (Santa Fe, N.Mex.: The Sunstone Press, 1975).

**Section Themes.** The oldest generation we interviewed for *Las Mujeres* were often farm women and rural women who had grown up speaking regional New Mexican Spanish. Isolated from mainstream society, they were primarily responsible for the emotional and physical well-being of their families and neighbors. In section 1, "But I Remember," these women speak of the importance of the traditions and customs of their church and community. With little formal schooling, they also tell of working to obtain a better education for their children.

Home was the central work place for the Hispanas of section 1. The question of woman's place in the home grows most distinct, however, in section 2, "The Soul of the Home." More urban than the previous generation, these women began to work at paid employment in their late teens and early twenties. This experience prompted them to examine closely the nature of their responsibilities to their homes and families.

The desire for education mentioned by the women in section 1 gains prominence in section 3, "Little by Little." Coming of age during an era of increased educational and job opportunities for all women, these Hispanas have been the first generation to complete high school and attend college in any substantial numbers. Often they have been thwarted in this advancement by prejudice and poverty. While these women still regard their families as one of their primary responsibilities, most of them also consider their paid jobs or careers an important and necessary source of satisfaction in their lives.

The women of section 4, "A Lighted Fire," tend the embers of their foremothers' concerns for the welfare of the community through their own interest in social change. Some of these young women are concerned specifically with the problems and rights of Hispanic people; others are concerned with the advancement of women's opportunities; however, all of them are determined that social change should come about, and the majority see themselves as working directly to create changes which will better the lives of Hispanas, Hispanos, and all people.

**Some Final Thoughts.** As noted above, oral history offers an opportunity to learn from people whose experience has been eclipsed in standard history books. In compiling these interviews, our own concept of social change has been broadened. We had long been aware that the institutions of our society can be influenced and changed through organized activities such as party politics, lobbying, strikes, picket lines, petition drives, marches, and boycotts—actions which are public, highly visible, and recognizably political. Learning about Louisa Vigil's determination to obtain an education for her children or the way Emma Gonzales and her husband divide family responsibilities has made us realize that social change also occurs through actions which are individual, private, and often very quiet. These life stories negate simplistic attempts to define human history as a time-line of famous leaders and great events. Oral history leads to an appreciation of the ways in which everyday actions may contribute to the shaping of our world.

To the three of us, these oral histories have had another special value. As we listened to the tapes we had collected, we were again and again impressed by the unique and often divergent voices we heard. These voices sharpened our realization that this book cannot make a definitive statement about the culture of southwestern *mujeres*. Culture changes with each generation, and its impact upon individual women also varies. What these voices tell us is that the experience of these women—women who have often been stereotyped—is, in fact, richly diverse.

The voices speaking here record only a part of the experience of New Mexican Hispanas, but by speaking, they have transformed their experience into history.

# Prologue

This book of oral histories was compiled by three women from three distinct cultural backgrounds. In the statements that follow, we have set down something of our own histories and the ways in which they led to this work.

**Yvonne Tixier y Vigil.** I am a Chicana. I call myself a Chicana, but it has taken me a long time to figure out who I am. Time spent talking with my grandmother, asking her, "What was it like in the old days?" Time spent talking with my friends and with my students at the University of Albuquerque, asking them, "What is important in our lives? How are things different for us now?"

For many years I had known that I was not *Anglo*. * But if I called myself Spanish or Mexican, my father's sister would haul out her family tree and talk to me firmly about my French grandpa and great-grandpa. If I called myself French or went with friends from mainstream America, there would be my grandma, scowling and saying, "*¿Porque no vas con la Raza? Estos Americanos no sirven.*" (Why don't you go with your race? These Americans aren't worth anything.)

Another reason it has taken me so long to figure out just where I belong is that when I was growing up, women, including Chicanas, did not talk about their identity. Because of this silence my own questions seemed petty and hard to verbalize. It was not until other women, braver than myself, voiced their wonderings about where we all belong culturally that my own questions began to surface.

When this happened, in the early 1970s, I started talking about "my problem" and started searching for books and stories about Hispanic women. Much to my surprise, I found that in books, only Hispanic men struggled with conflicts, whether internal or external. Although I could understand these male voices, try as I might, I could not identify with them. What about me? What about women? What were our problems? What were our lives?

There was little or nothing written about *la mujer* in the ethnic novels I read. When she did appear, it was as a mythological, faceless, submissive, helping, supporting, no-real-life-to-her woman. She was just there. I did not think of myself as a "just there" sort of person.

Reading about these women left me nowhere. There was no depth to

* *Anglo* = non-Hispanic, white American; sometimes, more narrowly, Anglo Saxon Protestant.

them. What were they thinking or dreaming while they made the *tortillas*, cooked the *frijoles*, or prayed their beads? None of these women were me or my friends. My *tortillas* never turn out round. My beans make gas, and my prayers aren't usually said to a rosary. Did this mean I was not a Chicana? Where, I wondered, could I read about myself? Where could I read about my family? What sorts of experiences did Chicana women share? What differences separated us from each other and from that mythological woman in the novels? Where could I find a book about us? Or would we have to make our own?

These were my thoughts at the time that I began to talk with my friends Nan and Kyle about the differences and similarities in our families and cultures. Out of our discussions and questions came a determination to get down on paper a glimpse of the lives of Hispanic women of several generations.

My grandmother, Louisa Vigil, was the first woman I interviewed. I had always been curious about her. She lived in northern New Mexico, in Bueyeros, in a house with a wood stove and an outdoor toilet. She had been old even when I was a child—very old, very small, with countless wrinkles over her sharp-boned face. I wondered how she did her work, with no electricity, no running water. How had she raised my mother, my aunts, my uncles? How had she met my grandpa? Did she ever feel lonely?

As I went through high school, married, divorced, went to college, supported two children, moved back and forth, there never seemed to be time for asking my grandma those questions or listening to the answers. It was not until she was eighty-five that I sat down with her at the kitchen table and, as she rocked in her chair, drinking her coffee, asked the first questions in our search for the histories of New Mexican Hispanas.

**Nan Elsasser.** Not long after Yvonne and I met at the University of Albuquerque, we started asking each other many questions of the kind raised in this book. Our questions always led to discussions about what it means to be *Anglo* and what it means to be non-*Anglo* in the United States. The longer we talked, the more I began to see that, in spite of vast differences in their positions in the society, Jewish and Hispanic women may have certain important common experiences. As children, for example, both Yvonne and I lived in homes in which much of our parents' cultural heritage was repressed. For Yvonne, this meant that she was not taught to speak Spanish. For me—who was Jewish, but not *that* Jewish—it meant having to stay in the house on high Holy Days for reasons never explained. And now, for both of us, it means a continual questioning of who we are, where we are going, and where we have come from.

The women who ask these questions most often are those of us who have started to become assimilated into the American mainstream. The "fence walkers," Yvonne calls us. It's not the women who live in all-Jewish or all-Hispanic neighborhoods who ask these questions, but we cultural half-breeds who don't feel a part of either world.

So, in many ways, Yvonne and I began questioning the women in this book from similar vantage points. I would like to say something here about what I learned from their answers. Not from the answers of each woman individually, but bit by bit, from hearing many *mujeres* tell their stories.

One of the most valuable things I learned from the women we interviewed is that in a world that is cold for women and for minorities, each woman does her best to accommodate herself and prepare her family to face that world. And from generation to generation I saw these women reaching out to support each other in their individual struggles. Time and again daughters explained their mothers' actions by saying, "That's all she could do." Time and again mothers explain their daughters' lives by saying, "But everything's different now."

Listening to these women helped me to see my own mother in a different light, and when I went home one Thanksgiving, I spoke to her for the first time as another woman. Not to the mother who offered me a model of everything I didn't want to become, but to one more woman who had tried to do right by her family and by her society—trying also to forget that deep down, she didn't really feel *Anglo*, not in her heart and soul—and whom for so many years I had seen only as a chauffeur, cook, and companion to her husband and children. I still wonder what happened to the young woman who worked her way through college, joined the navy, and went to graduate school. I doubt I'll ever know and maybe she doesn't either. But I understand better now.

Next, I learned about belonging. As a single woman who has never lived more than seven years of her life in one town, I have listened to many a *viejita* talk about how her great-grandmother planted that tree over there or how her husband built the room her grandchildren sleep in. I've found that, for all of my wanderings, I am fascinated, alternately attracted and put off, by people who have lived in the same place for generations. Sometimes when I come home from talking with Josephine or Ida I think what a fool I am to keep chasing after a Ph.D. and the mobility it affords. When all's said and done, who will remember another third-rate dissertation? The only real thing to do is to cook up a batch of beans, and have a coffeepot that's always full and a warm kitchen that smells of the smells that identify you and your family. To put down roots, in other words. Of course, I can't make myself do that any more than I can become Simone de Beauvoir, but the pull is there, and the respect for a way of life I had never really considered before.

Finally, I started work on this book with my own set of stereotypes about Hispanic women. Many of them were positive—but stereotypes, nonetheless. One by one, those various stereotypes crumbled, as I learned that there is no such thing as "the Hispanic woman." There are women who begin careers after rearing large families. There are women who never work outside their homes. There are women who enjoy close companionships with their husbands, women who expect little from their husbands, and women who do not want husbands at all. There are women who share my values, frustrations, and joys and others who want to "fix me up" with a "nice, steady man." With each of the women interviewed, I discovered both separations and bonds; but in the course of the work, I gained understanding of our separations and an increased appreciation of our bonds.

**Kyle MacKenzie.** It's hard for me to find the right words for this statement because basically I feel that my words have very little place in this book. When Yvonne read the draft of the first completed chapter, she said, "I like it. It makes me feel calm. It makes me feel at home." Well, I like it too. I like it so much that I've spent month after month listening to and writing down the words of Hispanic women. But it doesn't make me feel calm and it doesn't make me feel at home. In fact, very often, having a part in this book has made me feel uncomfortably like an intruder. I wanted to shrink into a very small corner where no one would notice me, but where I could still hear the stories.

That's one reason I've worked on this book—because I like stories, especially stories about women. I like hearing about the horse-drawn school bus that Josephine rode to school, or about the afternoon when Ana was so busy fishing that she forgot to mind the cows and they all ran away.

I like stories and I like words. I like true words. I like different words. I like words that come fresh and clean off women's lips. Words that take me places. Words that spill into phrases, images, and ideas I never encountered before. I like old words too. I like words that capture feelings and relationships as they repeat themselves from generation to generation. Words like grandma, mama, *mi'jita, hermana.* I like women's stories and I like women's words. That's my first reason.

I have another reason. This reason begins with my grandma's bean pot. My grandma's bean pot is round and glazed and brown and white with a small handle at the neck and a flat plain knob on the top. My grandma used to cook beans in that pot every Saturday night. She's dead now, and her bean pot sits in my kitchen. It has traveled eighty years and a couple of thousand miles from Hampton, Maine, to Albuquerque, New Mexico—but it's empty.

It's empty because somehow when my family moved from Maine to Montana to New York, we forgot the bean recipe. Somehow, in striving to become worldly and sophisticated, we left it behind with the broad New England *a*'s and the pickle barrel in the pantry. We lost it as we'd lost the Scottish burr and the haggis recipe years earlier. And when I was a little girl I didn't listen to tales of the Loch Ness monster or stories of my great grandma farming while my great-grandpa worked on a whaling boat. No, when I was young, I listened to Baby Snooks. I read Little Lulu. I wore bows on my braids like the girl on the Sunbeam bread label, and I tried my best to grow up just like Brenda Starr. For the most part I succeeded and, for the most part, so did thousands of other women. And today, when we look around us for our women's heritage, we find ourselves confronted by that bland, healthy, smiling mother and daughter of us all—the American woman clutching an empty bean pot. Well, I think of all those empty bean pots and I get scared. Scared that, like my grandma's recipe, the stories of women will be lost—that if we don't listen now, it will be too late. Too late to hear and preserve the stories of living *Anglo* women, Black women, Native American women, Asian women, Hispanic women, and the women of earlier times who still live in their memories. So I have listened to and recorded the conversations of New Mexican Hispanas, in order that their stories may be preserved and shared.

DECEMBER 1979

# LAS MUJERES

*To Delilah Padilla and Shirley Barefield,*
*who fought successfully to ensure equal rights*
*for themselves and other women prisoners.*

*(Barefield v. Leach, 1975)*

# ONE:
# BUT I
# REMEMBER

*No lloro,
pero me
acuerdo.*

I don't cry,
but I
remember.

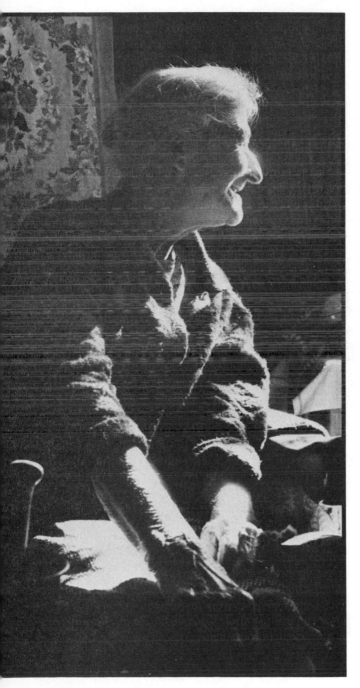

Old Hispanic
women of
New Mexico
look back upon
a tradition
of hard
work in an
inhospitable
land, and
responsibility
for family
and community.
Louisa Vigil,
at left,
reared
her eight
children in a
primitive
rural
environment,
but managed
to send
them all to
school.
At right,
Juanita
Sedillo,
eighty-three,
is a semi-
retired
*curandera*
(healer).
*Curanderas*
and midwives
were vital
to communities
that had no
other medical
care.

Like many other rural Hispanas of her generation, Andreita Padilla, shown at left on her patio, still likes to string her own *chiles*. In the old village of Los Padillas where she lives, near Albuquerque, she is a frequent visitor at the Senior Citizens' Center. There she enjoys chatting with friends such as those pictured at right, and, especially, dancing to the accordion player's lively renditions of Hispanic folk tunes.

Josephine Turrietta brings vigor to each of her many activities, whether working in the church or at her paid employment, helping strangers who are in need, or celebrating an ordinary meal with neighbors and family. Below, she demonstrates a crucial point in the making of tortillas for two attentive neighborhood children. Top right, the children gather at the table with Josephine and husband Frank Turrietta, their daughter, and their son-in-law. Bottom right: Frank and Josephine Turrietta in the garden of their home at Los Padillas.

**W**E HAD GONE to look for the *viejitas,** the women who know the secrets and the *cuentos* (stories) of the past. Through their thoughts and memories, we hoped to gain a better understanding of each living generation of *mujeres*.

The oldest women we interviewed had grown up at the turn of the century, when New Mexico was a Spanish-speaking territory. The youngest members of this generation were born in 1918, on the eve of the First World War. While some of these women came from the old Hispanic *barrios* of Albuquerque, the majority of them were from the rural communities, small mountain villages, and towns of the Rio Grande valley. These women have lived most of their lives in Spanish-speaking communities and have retained many Hispanic customs. They still butcher their own goats, string their own *chiles*, and celebrate Christmas with gifts of homemade *tamales* and *biscochitos* (anise cookies).

With few natural resources, New Mexico is an area in which it has long been difficult to make a living. During the early years of this century, both farming and housework required hard physical labor and included tasks for children as well as adults. And at an early age, Hispanas began to learn the chores of survival. "I don't think we played much in those days," said one woman, now in her seventies. "We had a lot of work to do at the ranch. I had to clean the house, make the meals, wash the dishes, sew and embroider."

For many women of this generation, school was a luxury. The real skills they were expected to need when they grew up were those they learned at home, and few of the women we interviewed had gone to school beyond the eighth grade. "I wanted so badly to be a teacher," one woman recalled. "When I was small, I used to put my three little dolls up, and I'd say to my sister, 'Let's teach the kids how to read.' But still my mother and father said I had to stop after the eighth grade.† There wasn't a high school close to us, and they didn't want me to go on the bus."

---

\* For Spanish words and expressions not translated into English in the text, or requiring further explanation, see the glossary on pages 155–156.

† In the early twentieth century, many beginning teachers in rural areas had no more than an eighth grade education; however, they attended teachers colleges during the summer months.

The Catholic Church has held a position of special importance in the lives of most *viejitas*. Many women in this age group still attend church three or four times a week and have vivid memories of their first Holy Communion. "On my first Holy Communion, I couldn't eat anything until I went to Mass, no water or anything. The Communion was in Spanish and I was dressed up all in white, with a cross. Then, afterwards, my mother made a big *fiesta* for all the family, and she told me, 'Don't run out in the street. Don't say bad words. Not anything. You have to be very quiet because you have Jesus in your soul.' That was great."

Religious celebrations, such as first Holy Communion feasts and festivals for patron saints, were the major entertainment in rural areas. "The church was our only entertainment then," said a woman of sixty-one. "We weren't allowed to go out with boys in those days. But May was Mary's month, and we had a whole month of holy rosary. During October, too. That was entertainment, because a whole bunch of girls would go to church together."

Most towns also held community dances. The young women who attended these dances were usually carefully chaperoned by their parents or older brothers and sisters. Often they were not allowed to talk privately with the young men they met, and could only become acquainted *con cartas* (through letters). "We didn't know each other before we got married. We wrote each other letters, that's all. We didn't date or anything like that. Only letters, and then we were husband and wife."

By the age of seventeen, most of the women had married. Going straight from their fathers' to their husbands' houses, they moved from being daughters to being wives and mothers, with little, if any, time in between. Birth control information was rare in those times, and the Catholic Church encouraged women to have large families. "We had eight children. That's how many God gave me," said Louisa Vigil, whose interview opens this section. Many women from this generation shared her attitude, viewing the size of their families as a matter beyond their province.

Louisa Vigil also reported that "the womans didn't work in

those days. The mans were supposed to marry that girl and take care of her." However, Louisa Vigil has spent her life working, as have most of these women, both for family and community. For country women, work was seldom a salaried job. More often it was the work of growing and preparing food, of making *adobes* and plastering houses with mud, of making their children's clothes for school and teaching them the hymns and prayers of the church, of delivering babies and treating sicknesses with herbs and patience. In almost every town there were one or two women who, in addition to working in their own homes, served other families in the community as *curanderas* (healers), *parteras* (midwives), and schoolteachers.

In spite of the importance given to women's work at home, approximately half of the *viejitas* we interviewed had also worked at paid occupations before and after marriage. These were generally city women, who had held jobs as maids, waitresses, and sales clerks, or who worked in small family businesses. Most often they considered their work a means of making financial ends meets, rather than a satisfying career. Two of the younger women we interviewed had worked in government programs, one as a clerk, the other as a community worker. Here they felt they were able to deliver valuable services to their friends and neighbors.

The six women speaking in this section tell us of their girlhood. They talk about the work they have done as farmers, wives, and mothers, *curanderas*, midwives, and participants in community activities. Describing their lives today, they also mention change and the problems of old age. Together, their stories create a sense of the endurance, strength, and vitality of New Mexican Hispanas of the past.

# Louisa Vigil

Louisa Vigil, Yvonne Tixier y Vigil's grandmother, was born on a ranch in northern New Mexico in 1890. Raised by her grandparents in Colorado, she was married in 1907, and moved to her husband's ranch, sixty-four miles from Clayton, New Mexico, the nearest town.

Louisa Vigil was the first woman interviewed for *Las Mujeres*. At eighty-seven, she is the matriarch of her family. A woman with strong ideas and a wealth of practical knowledge, she is regarded as the family advice-giver and chief storyteller. Despite the respect her words command with her family, Louisa Vigil felt ill at ease in talking about her life to her granddaughter. The repeated questions of the granddaughter and the often reluctant answers of the grandmother reveal the difficulties of two women trying to understand each other's lives and thoughts across a gulf of fifty years.

**YTV**: HOW OLD ARE YOU, GRANDMA?

**LV**: Eight-five *¡y que quieres?* (and what do you want?)

**YTV**: Eighty-five. Where did you come from?

**LV**: From home.

**YTV**: From home! But whereabouts is home?

**LV**: *Quítate, quítate.* (Leave me alone. Stop it.)

**YTV**: Grandma, *hábleme. Hábleme. ¿Porqué no quiere hablar conmigo?* (Talk to me. Talk to me. Why don't you want to talk to me?)

**LV**: *¿Cómo sé hablar contigo?* (How do I know how to talk to you?)

**YTV**: But I want to know. *Yo quiero saber todo* (I want to know everything). Where did we come from? What did great-grandpa do? What was it like when you were little?

**LV**: We come from Mora, but that was a long time ago, before my papa was born. He was born in Trinidad, Colorado, and he lived in Colorado, and he worked there in the mines, or where they're cleaning the gold. Refinery, I guess.

**YTV**: *¿Y qué pasó con tu mamá?* (And what about your mother?)

**LV**: Well, *mi mamá se murió desde que yo tenía dos años.* (My mother died when I was two.) So I went to live with my grandma and my grandpa. My father got married again, but I stayed with my grandma.

**YTV**: What was your grandma like?

**LV**: What was she like? She was my grandma. That's all.

**YTV**: That's not all, Grandma. What about the stories? Remember, you used to tell me about the stories your grandma told you, the stories about *brujas* (witches) and *el chivato* (the goat man).

**LV**: *No quiero hablar de las brujas* (I don't want to talk about witches).

**YTV**: I remember you told me about the man who asked this woman who was a *bruja* to take him to see the *casa de brujas* (witches' house).

**LV**: Yes, and she promised if he won't say nothing they could go. But when they got there, it was full of *brujas* and *brujos* (male witches) and the man opened his mouth—*¡Ave María Purísima* (Holy Virgin Mary)! *El chivato*, he put his tongue in the man's mouth.

**YTV**: Ugh, that'll teach him to stay away from *brujas*. What else? Did you go to school?

**LV**: Of course I went to school.

**YTV**: Oh, you did? They had schools in those days?

**LV**: Of course they did. I went to the sisters, the Sisters of Charity, since I started.

**YTV**: Did you go all the way through high school?

**LV**: No, just to the fifth grade.

**YTV**: How come you learned English so well? Did you speak English at home, or just Spanish?

**LV**: No, no, just what I learned in school. At home I spoke Spanish.

**YTV**: What else did you do when you were young? What did you do for entertainment?

**LV**: Go to the dances. That's all. We used to go to the dances.

**YTV**: *¿Qué clas?* (What kind?)*

**LV**: *Pues qué clase, pués bailes bonitos, honestos. Tocaron la guitarra y bailaron hasta las dos de la mañana.* (What do you mean, what kind? Pretty dances, honest dances. They played the guitar and danced until two in the morning.)

**YTV**: *¿Qué su papá y su mamá estuvieron conusted?* (Your father and mother were with you?)

---

* *Clas* and *clase* are used interchangeably in New Mexico, with *clas* as the preferred term. The accustomed usage, elsewhere, is *clase*.

**LV:** No, my stepmother. She used to go. She liked to dance, and she used to go. But that was later. That was after we moved to New Mexico. We moved to the ranch in Bueyeros. My father had a bunch of sheep and cows he took care of. Then he moved to Clayton, and he was the jailer there in Clayton. He was a jailer until the Republicans got out and the Democrats came in. He was a Republican.

**YTV:** What about dating? Did you ever date? Did you have a sweetheart before you got married?

**LV:** No, not much. Well, we couldn't in those years. We had the strict parents. They were just watching over us. I didn't have no sweetheart. *Lo único* sweetheart *que tuve era tu granpa.* (The only sweetheart I had was your grandpa.)

**YTV:** How old were you when you got married?

**LV:** Eighteen.

**YTV:** Eighteen? Well, why did you get married?

**LV:** Why did I get married? *¿A dónde más querrías que me fuera?* (Where else could I have gone?) I didn't have no home. I was with my grandpa and my grandma; and she died. She passed away, and then I didn't have nowhere to go. I had my father, but I didn't want to stay with my stepmother. So I decided to get married right away. Your grandpa didn't have any money, but he had his ranch in Bueyeros. He had his cows. He had his horses.

**YTV:** What did you do after you got married? Did you live with his family?

**LV:** Just for a few days, while they made my house. Then we moved to the ranch in Bueyeros.

**YTV:** How many children did you have?

**LV:** Eight. That's how many God gave me. The oldest died. They both died, George and Beatriz. Then, when your Aunt Bea was born, we named her after the other little girl, Beatriz.

**YTV:** What did you do for food? Did you grow the majority of your food and have your own cows?

**LV:** Yes, we planted some, the vegetables and all those things. Flour and other things, they got from Clayton.

**YTV:** When did you move to Clayton?

**LV:** When your Aunt Bea was big enough to go to school. I told your grandpa, "I don't want to stay here anymore. I'm going to town and take my children to school. I don't want them to be raised like *tontitas* (dummies)." So grandpa used to move us in every fall. It was a two days' ride then. We'd leave at four o'clock in the morning. We'd stop at noon to feed ourselves and the horses, then we'd camp out at night sleeping under the wagon. We'd get to Clayton at five o'clock the next evening. It was sixty-four miles. But that's all.

**YTV:** Don't say that grandma. Tell me, what's the difference between now *y antes* (and then)? Was it better then?

**LV:** Yes, yes.

**YTV:** Why?

**LV:** I guess because I was young and just started to live. *No había tanto dinero como hay ahora pero el tiempo muy a gusto.* (We didn't have a lot of money the way they do now, but times were good.)

**YTV:** Well, what about big families? Did everybody have big families?

**LV:** Well, I guess they did. *Bueno, pues entonces no había—* to prevent them. (Then, there was no way to prevent them.)

**YTV:** But if there were, you wouldn't have used it anyway.

**LV:** Well, I don't know, Yvonne, because it was a sin for a person to do that in those years.

**YTV:** Would you change anything, Grandma? Would you do anything different now if you were young?

**LV:** I don't know. Might. I don't know. Could.

**YTV:** Would you get a job?

**LV:** Yes.

**YTV:** Did you ever think of working when you were young?

**LV:** The womens didn't work at that time. The man was supposed to marry that girl and take care of her.

**YTV:** What were your duties as a housewife? Did you feel that if you got married you had to stay home and raise kids *y es todo* (and that's all)?

**LV:** Yes, we didn't go out. Even when times were rough I never worked for nobody, just what I had to work for my house. Oh, I went out when we traveled in the wagon, the whole family. We liked to go from one place to another and have a good time, but we didn't go to work. Your grandpa never did let me work for nobody. He always had work, and we never did have really bad times.

**YTV**: You always got the kids to school?

**LV**: Yes.

**YTV**: They went the whole time and you didn't find it hard to get them clothed?

**LV**: No, your grandpa was always working and whatever he would get, we would manage. He'd always make a garden and plant something and take care of his cattle. We had the meat and the pigs and the *frijoles*. Even during the Depression, he worked in the grocery store.

**YTV**: What about divorce, Grandma? No one got divorced then, did they?

**LV**: No, the man had to be very mean so the lady could have a divorce—and still some men were so mean and the lady just suffered what she had to suffer. *No como ahora. Ahora son puros divorciados* (Not like now. Now everybody is divorced.)

**YTV**: *¿Y qué otra cosa* (and what else), Grandma?

**LV**: *No sé otra cosa. ¿Qué otras cosas quieres que te diga? ¡Ya me confesaste!* (I don't know anything else. What do you want me to say? I've confessed myself!)

# Juanita Sedillo

Juanita Sedillo, eighty-three, lives about six miles south of
Albuquerque in a small town just west of the old road to Mexico.
Juanita Sedillo is a *curandera*. She treats patients for bodily illnesses
such as colds, stomachaches, arthritis, and flu, as well as for
emotional states, such as shock or fright.

Since the Mexican conquest, *curanderas* have held an important
place in the Hispanic community. Well versed in the uses of plant
medicine, they were often the only people in the community with
medical skills. *Curanderismo* has traditionally been open to
Hispanic women, and many *curanderas* have also served their towns
and villages as midwives—just as Juanita Sedillo has done.

With the modernization of Hispanic society, as well as the
increased availability of hospitals and conventionally trained doctors,
the number of *curanderas* in New Mexico is steadily decreasing.
It was Juanita Sedillo's awareness of this decline that prompted her
to talk with us. Speaking in the colloquial Spanish of New Mexico,
she expressed an equal faith in her special power over ills of the body
and the mind, but admitted that her own old age is beyond her cure.

A free translation into English follows the Spanish.

¿CUÁNTOS AÑOS TENGO YO? ¡Ni sé! No los alcanzo contar en
todos los dedos. Ochenta y tres. Y que me muero y no me muero
y allí estoy. Y me prendo otra vez como tábano. ¿Qué no?

La vida mía fue muy triste, muy pesada. A nosotros nos
tenían en un rancho y pues allí estábamos sembrando, escar-
dando. Nos ponían a escardar. La otra hermanita me decía,
"Vamos a sentarnos debajo de aquel árbol que al cabo no nos
mira mi papá." Y yo me sentaba. No más venía mi papá y nos
daba con el chicote. Entonces sí escardábamos, ¡pom! ¡pom!
Eso fue la vida de nosotros. Íbamos con mi abuelita que nos en-
señara chistes o molestar a mi abuelito. Nos rodiábamos de mi
abuelito y se ponía a echarnos más chistes pero le hacíamos
males. Lo jalábamos de los cabellos y allá andamos haciéndole
miles de males. Y luego nos pegaba. "¡Carajas!" nos decía.

Esa es la vida de los chiquitos, ¿no? Estar con los abuelitos para
que le digan a uno chistes o se ponen a rezar. Eso sí no nos gustaba.
Ya de que se ponían a rezar el rosario y oraciones hasta que nos
dormíamos. Esa fue la vida de nosotros de crearnos allá en el
rancho con los abuelitos.

Salíamos del rancho cuando íbamos a la escuela. Sí, salíamos de ese desierto. Nos íbamos a Feibro. Daban clases en inglés, no más. Pero ya después me vine aquí a Cuchillo y nos enseñaban en español. Bueno, mis tíos nos enseñaban en español, ¿no ves? Nosotros aprendimos el español con mis tíos, con mi papá. Todas, todas sabemos el español.

Muy bonito porque ahora ya hay mucha gente, los hijos pues, que no saben el español. ¿Porqué no les enseñan en los dos idiomas? Les enseñan el inglés y luego la de ellos la van echando para un lado. Uno de los bisnietos míos sabe muy bien todo en español y el otro no quiere. ¡No quiere! Y le dicen, "Háblale a la Grande en español porque ella no sabe el inglés." "I can't," dice.

Mis abuelitos no sabían leer ni escribir ni nada pero sabían curar muchas enfermedades. Mi abuelita, la mama de mi mamá era curandera. Nosotros no conocimos doctores. Ellas nos curaban y sanábamos. Nos daba fiebres o nos daba "flu" de sangre o cualquier mal que nos daba, nos curaban con yerbas y sanábamos.

De allí aprendimos poquito nosotros. De las bisabuelas y luego las abuelas y allí vienen nuevas y de allí viene siendo toda la historia, ¿no ves? Así pasó conmigo. También aprendí a curar y a asistir criaturas de una señora de Montecello; era curandera y era partera.

Comencé desde el 1930, el 1931. Una mujer allí en el rancho donde vivíamos estaba muy mala y vino el vecino por mí y le dije, "Pues yo no sé." No sabía nada todavía pero me fui. Estaba muy mala de pulmonía. "¿Sí, pues qué le voy a hacer yo? No sé pero voy a hacerle la lucha." Dios quizás me dijo, "Bate el mentolate con canela." Baté el mentolate con canela y le unté y luego le puse un trapo caliente. ¡Se le quitó pulmonía! Muy extraño. Quizás Dios me puso en la mente que le hiciera ese remedio a esa mujer.

Y entonces me enseñé a sacar plebe y seguí. Lo que curo más es empacho. Es lo que vienen más,—empachados, sospendidos o ya con un dolor en un lado o con dolor de cabeza. Por el empacho les sobo el estómago. Luego les jalo el cuero y luego les doy la medicina y de allí echan el empacho. Lo mismo cuando es inflamación. No más les sobo allí poquito y luego les doy una clase de medicina que se disvuelve esa clase de inflamación. Con puras yerbas medicinales, yerbas mexicanas hace uno las medicinas y con eso tiene. Por eso las creó Dios.

Cuando asistía mujeres no más les daba una poquita de pimienta en una poquita de agua para que les diera empuje. O pasas. Las hierve uno y luego el caldo también les da 'pujo. Después pa' que se curara les daba hipazote o chimajá, tu sabes pa' que se limpiara. Y para tener hijos he curado muchas. Se les calienta la matriz. Tienen mucho frío en la matriz. Mientras esté helado no hay nada. Yo he curado muchas pero hay veces que el hombre es el que le falta.

Curo de todos—mujeres, hombres, nenes. Susto, casi es lo que curo más ya. A este mío, Siriaco, tenía la sangre muy livianita. Cuando estaba en el army le hicieron mal y me escribió y me dice, "Mamá, tengo el mal aguao"—porque así le dice—"mándame la medicina." Pues ya le mandé oshá y unos granitos de sal tostados. No más agarras oshá y sal y los escupes todos y luego les envuelves.

Muchos no creen en el ojo. Pero que les hacen, sí. Y a veces sin darse cuenta. Una vez estaba mi'jo en el army. Y allí estaba mi primo Iginio. Todos los días me decía de Siriaco que buena suerte que estuviera en el army, jugando. Yo no sentí que me dió coraje pues él siempre me decía. Pero quizás ese día me dió coraje pues el cuento es que se quedó él sin habla. Se rió mi tía y me dijo, "agarra nuez y échale en la lengua." Sí agarré nuez y "saca la lengua" le dije. Le eché. Luego habló. "¡Que bárbara!" después decía mi primo. "No le hagas nada a mi prima porque te deja sin habla."

He curado de todo. Hasta Albuquerque voy todo el tiempo. De allá de Albuquerque vienen por mí. He enseñado a otras. Les digo que usen éste por el empacho y tal por el otro y lo que sea. Y ahora ya casi no curo. No más que vienen aquí les digo que vayan a mi nuera porque ya mi nuera ya cura.

Lo que me dicen a mí que como no me curo yo. Pues sí me curo y me hago todos los remedios que sé que sean buenos pero Dios quizás no quiere que sane. De aquí a mañana me muero.

How old am I? I don't even know! I don't have enough fingers and toes to count. Eighty-three. I think I'm dying, and I don't die, and here I am. I light up again like a firefly, no?

My life was very sad, very tough. We were raised on a ranch, and we spent our time planting, hoeing. They'd have us hoeing, and my little sister would say, "Let's sit down under that tree. Papa won't see us." And I'd sit down. As soon as we sat down, my father would come with a whip. *Then* we'd hoe! Wham! Wham! That was how we lived.

We used to go with my grandmother, who told us jokes, or go and bother my grandfather. We'd gather around my grandfather, and he'd begin to tell us more jokes, but we'd harass him. We'd pull his hair and torment him. Finally he'd hit us. *"Carajas"* he'd call us.

But that's the life of a child, no? To be with your grandparents so they can tell you jokes. Or while they pray. We sure didn't like that. They'd say the rosary with us, and then go on to other prayers, until we fell asleep. That's how it was growing up on the ranch with our grandparents.

We left the ranch to go to school. We left that desert and went to Felbro. The classes there were all in English. Later I came to Cuchillo and they taught me in Spanish. My uncles also taught me Spanish, see? We learned Spanish from our uncles, from our dad. And we all know Spanish.

That was nice because now a lot of people, children, don't know Spanish. Why don't they teach them in both languages? They only teach them in English, and little by little, they lose their own language. One of my great-grandchildren knows Spanish real well, but the other one won't even try. He doesn't even want to speak Spanish! They tell him, "Speak Spanish to your great-grandma, because she doesn't know English." "I can't," he says.

My grandparents didn't even know how to read or write. But my grandmothers knew how to cure many illnesses. My grandmother, my mother's mother, was a *curandera.* We never saw a doctor, but they would treat us, and we would get better. If we got a fever or flu, or whatever we caught, they took care of us with herbs and we got better.

From them we all learned a little about medicine. From our great-grandmothers and then our grandmothers. There's always new *curanderas* who teach the next generation, and that's how the art continues, see? That's how I became a *curandera.* I also learned to heal and deliver babies from a woman in Montecello who was a *curandera* and a midwife.

I began in 1930, 1931. A woman on the ranch where we lived was very ill, and a neighbor came to me for help. I said to him, "Well, I don't know." I didn't know anything [about healing], but I went. She was very sick with pneumonia. [I thought to myself], "Yes, but what can I do for her? I don't know, but I'll try hard." Perhaps it was God who told me, "Mix menthol with cinnamon." I mixed them, and rubbed it on her, and then put a hot towel on her. She got better. Strange. Maybe God put it into my mind to make that remedy for that woman.

Later I learned to deliver babies, and I kept on. What I treat most often is *empacho* (stomachache). Most people who come to see me have digestive problems, or a pain in their side, or a headache. For *empacho*, I massage their stomachs and pull their skin. Then I give them the medicine, and from that, they get rid of the *empacho*. The same for an inflammation. I massage the area a little bit, and then I give them medicine to dissolve the inflamation. I make my medicines solely from herbs, Mexican herbs. That is all you need—that is the reason God put all those herbs on the earth.

When I delivered babies, I gave the women a bit of pepper dissolved in water to help them push. Or raisins. You boil them and then use the broth. It helps them push. Afterwards, I gave them tea made from *hipazote* or *chimajá* to clean them out. I've also helped a lot of barren women have children. You have to warm their womb. Their wombs are cold, and as long as they're cold they can't conceive. I've helped a lot of women, but sometimes it's the husband who can't have children.

I've healed all kinds of people—women, men, children. Illness from fright is what I cure most. My son, Siriaco, had very weak blood. When he was in the army they put some kind of spell on him, and he wrote me to send him medicine. I sent him *oshá* and a few grains of roasted salt. All you need is *oshá* and salt. You spit on them, and then you wrap them up.

A lot of people don't believe in such a thing as the evil eye, but you can cast a spell, sometimes even without knowing it. Once when my son was in the army, my cousin Iginio began to tease me. He was always saying how lucky I was that Siriaco was in the army. Just teasing. I didn't even know that I was angry, because he used to tease me like that all the time. But I guess he got me mad that day—and the result was that he lost his speech. My aunt laughed and told me to get some pieces of nuts and put them on his tongue. I told him to stick out his tongue, and I covered it with the ground nuts. Then he could talk again. After that, my cousin would always say, "Don't bother her, because she'll leave you mute."

I have cured all types of illnesses. I've traveled all over, all the way to Albuquerque. People would come all the way from Albuquerque to get me to heal someone. And I have taught others. I tell them, "Look, this remedy is for this, and this one is for that, and so on." Now that I've taught others how to do it, I don't work much any more. When someone comes to see me, I send them to my daughter-in-law to be healed.

People ask me why I don't heal myself. Well, I try. I make all the medicines that I know are good. But maybe God doesn't want me to get better any more. Nothing guarantees that I'll be here tomorrow.

# Andreita Padilla

Each day Andreita Padilla goes back to her grade school in Los Padillas, to the room where, fifty years ago, she graduated from the eighth grade. Today, the old Los Padillas school has become a community center, and Andreita Padilla's classroom is a senior citizens' meal site. She and the other women and men usually arrive an hour or so before lunchtime to dance and talk together. Now the room once sternly ruled by a teacher bounces to polkas and *rancheros* played by an old man on the accordion.

It was here, in this classroom, that we first saw Andreita Padilla dancing with her friend Josefina Garza. Holding her friend in her arms, Andreita Padilla moved purposefully around the room, smiling and marking out the polka rhythms she'd learned so long ago with quick, determined footsteps.

Andreita Padilla is sixty-five and lives with her husband in Los Padillas. Married for fifty years, they have raised six children together and a number of grandchildren and great-grandchildren. In talking about her life, however, she skips over those long years of marriage and family responsibilities and goes directly back to the time when she was very young and the world "so big."

WHEN I WAS VERY SMALL, I didn't have no father but . . . here's one problem . . . I don't speak good English. *Mejor diga en* Spanish (it would be better if I told you in Spanish), but, then the people who read the book might not understand me. So? I was born about a week after my papa died. I didn't know my daddy at all. Then my mother got married with another man, and I don't know, maybe she had trouble with me because I wasn't his, but anyway, I was raised up by a grandmother in La Paloma. And she was an angel. She was an angel. I was very small—and oh, she was big—big, with a round face, all red; green eyes and big eyelashes. *Alemana* (German), my grandmother. So I helped her all I could because she was so good.

She was very, very poor. The floors of her house were made of *tierra* (earth), *soquete* (mud). We had a cow, but my grandmother she didn't have nothing to buy food for the cow. So we used to cut alfalfa. She'd say, "Let's go, *mi'jita* (dear daughter)." We'd go over to the ditch and we'd cut some hay and grass and all kinds of weeds. Then we'd bring them for the cow to eat. We'd feed the cow, and all week we'd have milk with *tortillas*, bread or *galletas* (biscuits). We drank that milk with *galletas* in the morning, we drank that milk at noon with *galletas* or *tortillas*, we drank that milk at supper with *galletas* and with *sopa*. We used to eat *frijoles* and *chile* too, corn, if somebody gave her corn. But most of all we drank milk, milk.

And she was very good to me, my grandmother. If I was sick, she would put garlic and onions on me. She used to give me volcanic oil, too. You drank it with sugar. It was kerosene oil to make the heart go, but we drank it and we didn't get poison or nothing. They sold it in green bottles.

My grandmother used to tell me about *La Llorona* too.* She said, "If you don't do these things, *La Llorona* will send you to learn how to behave."

And I'd say, "*La Llorona!*"

"The *Llorona*'s something like an animal. It has horns and big fingernails and if you're a bad little girl, it will go into you. So you'd better pray to the Lord, Mary, and Jesus, and if you go with God, God's going to take you on the good road. Then, you're going to be a nice little girl."

Then every night she'd kneel me down and if she was sick, I'd say *la bendición*. We'd kneel down near the bed and we'd pray. My husband says that I pray for all the world, and I do. I pray for anyone that needs help—rich, poor, sick, healthy.

I remember my *abuelita* and how good she was, but she was too old—eighty years old or ninety. *Muy viejita, pero siempre la quería mucho*. (Very old, but I always loved her very much.) So, I was happy, very happy. But then she died. My mother said, "Now that your grandma's died, you have to go with your other grandma." And that grandma was too strict, too strict.

She was *sorda*, deaf, and she couldn't see right. I sure do appreciate her this day, though, because she straightened me. She straightened me for the good road and she was good at that. With no father or mother maybe I could have gone wrong, but she kept me straight all the time. She kept me working all the time.

---

* *La Llorona* is a mythical figure who roams the countryside crying for her dead children; parents sometimes coerce their children into good behavior by threatening that *La Llorona* will take them. *La Llorona* also appears to drunkards as a beautiful woman. When neared, she turns suddenly to reveal the face of a hideous horse. Said to have cured many an alcoholic.

On Mondays we had to wash. We brought the water in from
outside. Even if there was snow, we'd clean a space by the well.
We'd get the water in a bucket and we'd bring it inside and we'd
put it in the tub. Then we'd start washing the clothes. We'd wash
them and right away we'd take them over to the stove and boil
them. Then we'd take them outside, wash them again and put
in the bluing. First the cold water and then the bluing. Oh! it was
so clean and so pretty, those sheets and the bluing water, and
those blouses and everything. I used to do all that. Then I'd hang
it up. I was too small to do it, but she made me, and I did it.

She made me do the cleaning too. I used to clean our little
room and paint it. I had to put a chair on a table so I could climb
up because the ceilings were too high. Then I took *yeso* and the
skin from the sheep and I painted all over that little room.* I
painted and I cleaned and I did everything. I still do everything.
I mopped this morning, and my husband said, "You already
mopped this morning?"

And I said "Yes!" I mopped and I dusted. Made my beds,
made my food—everything is made in my house. My grandma taught me this way, and I can't sit still, I have to go on this
way all the time.

Sometimes when we finished all the work, I'd play with my
friends. We'd jump rope, play hopscotch and sing and dance to
"*Naranja Dulce.*" We sang it like this:

| | |
|---|---|
| *Naranja dulce,* | Sweet orange, |
| *Limon partido,* | Halved lemon, |
| *Dame un abrazo* | Give me a hug |
| *Que yo te pido.* | Because I'm asking you. |

It was so pretty.

So we worked all the week long. This was my school over here,
but my grandmother was so strict she wouldn't send me. She'd
say, "Well, you're not going to school today, Monday. We have to
wash clothes." On Tuesday we'd have to iron. Wednesday, we'd
have to clean the floor with a scrub brush, a *cepillo.* Well, I came
to school Thursday and Friday, and that was all. Then, when I
came, the teachers didn't put me good attention, but it wasn't

* *Yeso* = gypsum; sulfate of lime used for whitening walls.

my fault. I kept on telling the teachers that my grandma wouldn't send me and I had to do what she said. God! I don't know how I learned. I can write Spanish and read it. I write in English, not very good, but I write in English and I read it. I guess God helped me because I couldn't come to school. I guess He said, "If she don't have no help, I'll help her." The teachers, they were all *Anglos*. There was no Spanish at all. It was hard, because when I needed to go to the bathroom, I didn't know what to say. I just put up my hand and I told them, you know, but it was hard. I thought, "Maybe if I try I can learn it. If I try to break my head learning it, I can understand it." And it wasn't too long to learn. But that's why I taught my family English, so they don't be so ignorant.

And those were the days of the week. The weekends were different. Of course, on Sundays we'd go to church, and she'd never let me do anything on Sunday. The mass was in Spanish. She couldn't hear it, but she liked to go to church. Afterwards, we'd go to some relatives' house. We'd walk and I'd hold her by the hand. You couldn't hear the cars. There was no cars.

We didn't work much on Saturdays, either. Every Saturday I had my bath. We washed our hair and we had our baths and we didn't use any soap at all. We used *amole*. It grows over there on the hills. We'd pick it for the root. We'd pick it, and then we'd smash it with the hammer and put it in the sun to dry. When we washed our hair, we'd use it with water, like powder. It made a lot of lather, *espuma*, bubbles. We washed our hair in the tub and it came out shiny, shiny, beautiful.

One Saturday—I remember I was about eleven or twelve—and *se empezó el tiempo* (I started my period). I got really scared. I didn't know what was happening. I thought I was dying. We were eating dinner, and I knew after we started eating she'd never let me get up until I'd finished, but I felt something.

"*Abuelita*, I have to go to the toilet, *excusado* (outhouse)." We had the toilet outside.

"How many times do I have to tell you when God's serving your food, you don't supposed to move."

She was about to spank me, and I didn't know what to say. So I just said, "Something's happening to me."

"Eat your food."

"I'm not hungry, I'm not hungry." And I came away from the

table and I didn't eat. This was Saturday, too, and she knew very
well I'd had my bath, but then on Sunday: "*Abuelita,* I want to
have a bath again."

"You're not going to have a bath. You had a bath yesterday.
You can have a bath Monday or Tuesday or some other day, but
not one day after another."

She came over to me and she knelt down and she saw a little
bit, then she said, "Well, no, you're going to have a bath."

"What happened?"

"Well, this is *tu tiempo* (your time)."

"What's *tiempo?*"

"Every lady has that. It's natural for every girl when they get
so many years. Some are thirteen, some are ten. You don't have
to worry."

So I think, "This is going to happen every month."

And you weren't supposed to get wet because you might swell
up and get an *enfermedad* (illness), or something like that. You
couldn't have a bath or walk without your shoes. They made us
settle down. They gave us volcanic oil and then, "Lay down.
Stay there." And they gave us more volcanic oil and put warm
rags on the stomach and on the back. Poor little old ladies, they
were so good, but they just didn't know. It was too bad, and I was
all alone, all alone. I found it all by myself with nobody to say it.

When I got to be thirteen or fourteen, my *abuelita* used to take
me to dances. There she'd stand, with me in the chair, and I
couldn't tell any of them No. It didn't matter if they were old or
young. "If you're going to dance with the young ones, you have
to dance with the old ones. If they're blind or not blind, *sordo* or
*mudo* (deaf or mute)."

The dances used to be down the road over there. That's where
I met my husband. I had another boyfriend first, but I don't think
he liked me. This one liked me. I didn't go with him long though,
just a little bit and I was never alone with him before we got mar
ried—not in the house, or to the corner. They wouldn't let us go
anywhere, and they wouldn't tell us anything, either. They only
said that girls weren't supposed to go with boys until they got
married, and not to trust the boys, but they didn't explain anything.

So after a little bit, my husband and I, we got married. I was so young when I got married. I was fifteen—and you know what I did? He was seven years older than me, old enough to be a man, and he used to go out, but I didn't care. He'd go out with another friend and as soon as he left, I'd go to my friends to play house. I'd get tired of playing with my friends, so I'd come home and start cooking beans. Then I'd go outside to play hopscotch, and I'd burn the beans. So I'd have to go and ask my mother, "Do you have any beans? I burned mine. I was playing hopscotch."

My husband and I had good times too. I remember when we first got married. I used to go racing with him. He had a horse and I had a horse. My horse's name was *Cuanco*. Well, my little horse used to run. We'd race and we'd race and I won. I was so happy. Oh! We used to have fun on the horses.

It was kind of hard, yes. We were raised in the poor days, but everything was so settled. Maybe it was better that way. Now I'm old, though, I don't remember any more of those things I've told you the house, and I've told you my grandma, and the next time my grandma, too. I've told you the school and my husband. I don't remember any more.

# Josephine Turrietta

When first interviewed, Josephine Turrietta worked as the assistant director of the Los Padillas Community Center. The center had been started in 1965 through a combination of federal funds and local know-how. "The rule when I was hired," said Josephine Turrietta, "was that you had to be from this area and you had to know the people's needs. Well, I've lived in Los Padillas thirty-five years so I had a pretty good idea of what people want."

Determining people's needs and working for their fulfillment is not a new job for Josephine Turrietta, but rather a goal she has striven toward in a number of paid and volunteer positions. When she was sixteen she got her first job, cleaning houses to help put her sisters and brothers through high school. In later years she and her husband served as *mayordomos* (caretakers) for the church; and she has since worked as a volunteer in many other church and community activities. "I've done a lot of good things in my life," she says, "and I will keep working and continue to fight for what I believe is right, and for my people.

I WAS TWELVE WHEN MY MOTHER DIED, and sixteen when my father died. There were eight of us. There were four older than me. Altogether we had two brothers and six sisters. It's hard when you lose your parents. We had uncles and aunts, but nobody said, "Let's take care of those kids." We just managed to stay together. Being that all of us were raised alone, we could have gone wrong, because there was no one to advise us, to discipline us. We had no one—none of the relatives on my mother's side or my father's side would come to our rescue. But us kids managed to stay together. Even now, we are real close.

Nineteen twenty-seven was the year my mother died, and the year the Depression started. She died very young. She was thirty-four. I really don't remember what she died of. All I remember is that it was pitiful. My dad didn't have money enough to bury her. He had to ask my aunt for money. She was a very rich woman, because my uncle was the first lawyer in New Mexico. She loaned him those gold pieces to bury her. There was no welfare, no Social Security, no nothing. We never heard of welfare. It was pitiful.

I remember that Christmas when mother died. My father was

working nights. People, I don't know who they were, came over to our house with boxes of oranges, apples, candy, and bread— something for us to eat because we didn't have nothing. We were poor and we were starving. I tell you, this is why I feel for those people who are poor. If I have money, and I see someone who's really having trouble, I let them have it. I don't even tell them, "Pay me back." Or I go to the grocery store and get them something. I do.

My father was a farmer and a private security police. He had about ten acres, which at that time was quite a bit of property. Part of the property was where the Southern Union Gas Company is now, and it went across the tracks on the other side of Griegos Street. We had to help my daddy cut hay, rake it, and bale it. You name it, we had to do it. We would go to bed at nine or ten, and then we would get up with the chickens. My father managed to hang onto that land while he lived, but we lost all of it because we couldn't pay the taxes after he died of a heart attack. He was a very good provider. He was a very good father.

Anyway, after my parents died I had to go to work. My older sisters had to go to work, too. I went to work for fifty cents a day, doing housework. I had to walk three miles each way. What could you buy with fifty cents nowadays? You can't buy nothing. I remember, my mother used to send me to the store—potatoes, you could buy a bag for fifteen cents, and hamburger for ten cents. Yes ma'am, I'm not kidding, you could bring home something. Today, they charge you fifty cents for a meat ball, I tell you—or they might not even let you in the door of the store for fifty cents.

My younger sisters went to school. They graduated from high school. I didn't get to go to high school. I did graduate from the eighth grade, though—that was in 1935–36.

My mother taught us how to speak English before we went to school. She spoke beautiful English. My father didn't know very much English. What he knew, he just picked up here and there. My mother taught us English at home so that when we went to school, we already knew our language. We spoke both Spanish and English at home.

I think people aren't speaking Spanish any more because the parents are lazy. That is putting it bluntly. I think that they should teach their kids Spanish because that language is the most beautiful thing. They shouldn't forget it. I am very proud that I can speak both.

My father used to subscribe for the Spanish newspaper, *El Nuevo Mexicano*. He used to get it from Santa Fe. I would get the paper, and I would go over it letter by letter. That's how I learned how to read Spanish. Now, I read it and write it, and nobody taught me.

I didn't date very much when I was young. I wasn't allowed to go out. My father was a very, very strict man. Now that I realize why, I'm happy that he was. If we went to the store or to our girl friend's house, or whatever, he would sit up and wait for us until we got home. He would want to know if somebody gave us a ride, who we had come home with, or why were we so late.

After we grew up and were eighteen, nineteen, and twenty, then we would go to dances. We would get together with our girl friends and walk to Griegos to the dance. It wasn't too far—we would walk down there and back. It was safer then than it is now. Boys then would respect you. Nice clean fun—not like today. Today, forget it. You can't even stick your head out of the window.

I didn't date until I was 'way past twenty-one. It used to make me feel very jealous because my older sisters and brothers would go as far as Santa Fe to a *fiesta* and I couldn't go. Then I started dating my first husband. I married the first time when I was twenty-three years old. It lasted eleven months—the man I married was a bum.

I had no experience whatsoever, no one to give me advice. The man I married had been in prison for stabbing his mother, by accident. He'd tried to stab his brother in a fight, but his mother got in the middle to separate them, and he stabbed her. She put him in jail.

He was an alcoholic. It was very sad. Sometimes I used to say, "¡*María Santísima, quítemelo!* (Blessed Mother, take him away from me!)." It was an obligation, and I lasted with him until God took him away.

I'll never forget the day I found him dead. *Era el día de San Juan* (it was St. John's feast day), and he hadn't come home. It was *fiesta* time, and I had been working, to try to make him ashamed that I had to go out and make a living. I came home, and he wasn't home. He was out somewhere dancing in the neighborhood. It was a very sad life for me, really. Anyway, I waited for him until three o'clock in the morning, then I decided to go out and look for him. Of course, the first thing that comes to a woman's mind is that maybe he is sitting with a woman. I was looking in windows. I could have gotten shot. I finally saw his black '35 pickup, and I looked into it. He was laying face down, with his hat on top of his body. I thought that he was dead drunk. I stuck my hand into his pocket to get out the key and drove home, not realizing that he was dead.

When I got home, I couldn't get him out of the pickup. I pulled and pulled, and I finally got him out, and got him on the bed. When I turned him over, I noticed that his mouth was over to one side with all this foam coming out. I went over to my mother-in-law's, and I told her, "Somebody must have killed your son. I just found him."

I was accused by my mother-in-law of murdering her son. She said I had poisoned him, so I went down to the sheriff's office and I said, "No way. I'm telling you the truth, that's how I found him." He died, really, of unknown causes. Like I said, he was a drunkard.

His family never did like me, because I wouldn't let them run all over me. The mother had already given him the deed to the property when he was building our house, and it was in his name only. So, when I went to make arrangements for the funeral, I told my in-laws to let me off at the bank. I went and talked to my lawyer, and I told him, "Here are the papers. You do what you have to do. They are accusing me of such and such. I just found my husband dead, and I want these papers cleared up." After I talked to the lawyer, I went on and finished making arrangements for the funeral. When I got home, I found my house ransacked. His people were looking for that deed. They couldn't do nothing. They couldn't take the property away from me. I sold it.

For four years I did housework, to support myself and pay for the funeral. It was murder. It really was. At that time, the funeral cost me eight hundred dollars, and his parents never helped me, not even his brothers or sisters. I had to pay for it all myself. Like I say, it was a very sad life.

I was a widow for four years, then I met my present husband.
He, too, was a widow. I met him at a dance, and he took to me
right away. He asked me to marry him, and I said yes. I like him
a lot.

I married a very religious man. He don't believe in going to
church every day, like some of them do, but he believes in doing
his Sunday obligation. He's a very good man, and he's been very
nice, very helpful. He had four kids himself when we got married—later we had Katie. He helped me do the washing, he helped
me do the cooking. When the kids were small and I used to bathe
them, he used to help me give baths to the kids and put them to
bed and everything. I think that's wonderful. I don't think a lot
of men would do that today. I doubt it. These young men, they
would rather leave their young wives at home to do all the work
while they go out and gallivant and find somebody else. There's
where the problems come in.

While the kids were still home together, we had fifteen acres
of land. We had a big orchard which had about two hundred and
fifty apple trees. We also had peach and cherry trees. We had
seven acres of watermelons, *chile,* tomatoes, and whatever. We
raised everything. We had two pickups. He would drive one and
I would drive the other. We would go peddling our produce both
in and out of town. We'd always work together. We really worked
hard. We also had cows, chickens, and pigs. I used to make cheese
and butter, gather the eggs, and get milk from the cow. We don't
have that much land now, just the land around our house. I'm
glad, because I don't want him to farm any more. It's too much
work. He's not getting younger anyway.

My old man and me, we've never had any problems. He's not
a jealous man and I'm not a jealous woman. When you're not
jealous, both of you can work together and do things together.

We had a big family, I guess. I would have liked more, but I
couldn't. This is why I get upset about this abortion. These girls
don't want the babies God gives them. What's wrong with these
girls today that don't want to be responsible for those babies?
God is wonderful and so big. He's got so much room in His heart
for everybody. He will provide. With Him, you're not alone. This
I know. This I know, because of when my daughter was so sick.
I pleaded, and I asked, and she survived. I do believe in Him very

strongly, because of what I suffered when my daughter was so sick. Because it was a big miracle that she survived. She was dying. Sometimes, I go to bed and can still see her on that bed in the hospital. Even now it makes me cry. This is why I pass it on to anybody, that God does put things on this earth for us to see, to look, and to hear. He sends us all of these kinds of examples. Yet we're blind. We're stubborn. We don't want to listen to Him, and then we wonder, "Why?" Every Sunday when I go to Mass, I still thank Him for sparing that daughter for me.

My daughter and I have always been close, maybe because she's the only one I had. As I said, I couldn't have no more kids. The doctor said that I couldn't carry any more babies so they fixed me up so I couldn't have any more. I really would have liked to have had another one, so she wouldn't have to be alone. Maybe we would have had a son.

But these kids today have different ideas. Everything is old-fashioned to them. They don't think like we used to. A lot of things have changed.

Take the church, for example. Years ago they used to have the San Isidro and Los Padillas *fiestas*. They used to have dances, processions, and, of course, Mass. It was really nice. People would invite people to their homes after Mass or during the *fiestas* to have all kinds of goodies. Just like for Christmas, we would really do the cooking because we knew that there was going to be a lot of people coming over to the house. We would bake chicken, roast beef, and pork, make *enchiladas*, bread pudding, and *posole*. We would make all of that good stuff. Now, everyone is a stranger. You go to Mass and that's it. Everybody goes home, goes out and does their yard work, or whatever. It is very, very sad.

In the old days, the church used to be the center of activities. We used to help clean the church and help give dinners for the different societies that would come into the church for meetings. Some of us used to cook Spanish food for the priests to serve to other priests when they had visitors. Everyone used to get involved.

We used to have what you call *mayordomos*. We were *mayordomos* for a year. You would have to be picked. A couple that were *mayordomos* would come to your house and ask you if you wanted to be the next *mayordomos*. If you said yes, then it was your turn to work in the church, collecting money from people to buy flowers, cleaning materials. In other words, *mayordomos* were really in charge of taking care of all the things in the church.

I've worked in the church all my life. I did more work before I started working as a cook at the school. When you have a job, you don't have as much free time to work in the church.

I've been working here at the community center for three or four years. I've learned an awful lot about people, working here, because you hear people's problems. You learn from them. For a year before I started working here, I volunteered for the senior citizens. You sit down with them and you talk, and you learn. You hear their problems. They tell you about being old, neglected. They feel sad. They feel unwanted and not loved enough. I'm telling you now, you learn what to do for people like that only if you talk to them.

I remember when I started working here, there was no heat. There was nothing. The building was just torn down completely. We were freezing. I told Lina, the head of the program, "Let's ask the county for money. Let's write a letter." She said, "Well, I never wrote a business letter." I told her that I would write it, and she could type it. I even hand-delivered it. In the letter, I stated that we had space available for a clinic, and room for other agencies to come in, if the building could be repaired. They finally sent us twenty-two thousand dollars—but not before we had painted the building ourselves. We donated money out of our checks, and I crocheted a blanket, which we raffled off and got eighty-five dollars. With that money, we painted the inside. We cleaned the floors on our knees. We even plastered. We didn't have help from nobody, not even our director. Of course, I might as well be honest about it, they got kind of peeved at us because we did what we did without getting permission. I told them that we had been to three meetings, and had asked for help, and they didn't give it to us.

Now we have the Head Start program, the senior citizens, and the maternity and infant care clinic from the university. We also now have the family health and the WEEK Program which provides milk, eggs, and cheese for the babies from three to five years old. All of these agencies came in within a year. Now, they tell us that there's no more funds to keep us. Me and Lina will soon be out of a job.*

I sit back like I am now, just talking, and I say to myself, my goodness, I consider myself very, very lucky considering all of the hardships that I have gone through, all of the sad things that has happened to me in my life, and I think how fortunate I am that I have been able to express myself, and that I have learned things by myself where I had nobody to teach me anything. I think it's a very beautiful thing when a person has within the ability to survive. I thank God.

* A few months after this interview, federal funds for the community center were cut and Josephine Turrietta's job was phased out. The programs she helped to get under way in her five years at the center, however, are still operating

# Susana Archuleta

In her sixty-three years of life, Susana Archuleta has had a variety of jobs. As a youngster, she got her first paying job during the Depression, in Franklin D. Roosevelt's National Youth Administration. Later she married, had children, and held jobs as a salesclerk and as a waitress. Today, she works in the Sandoval County Health Department. The work that has given Susana Archuleta the most satisfaction, however, is midwifery. For almost forty years she has worked as a part-time midwife, following in the footsteps of her Hispanic ancestors, the *parteras* who began practicing their craft in New Mexico more than three centuries ago.

I WAS BORN IN NEW MEXICO, on a farm up North in Mora County. I was the fifth of eight children. When I was very little, my dad moved us all to Wyoming. You see, he heard that they had free textbooks in Wyoming, while here in New Mexico the parents had to pay for the books. Daddy didn't have much money, and he felt that we all needed an opportunity for education. We left the farm—the animals, the machinery, everything—and he went to work in the mines up in Rock Springs, Wyoming.

To me, growing up in Rock Springs was a very beautiful experience. It was a little coal-mining town, and most of the people there were foreigners who had come over from Italy, or Greece, or Finland. Everybody spoke their own language but somehow the children understood each other.

We all went to school in a little one-room schoolhouse, that's where we learned English. The building was divided in two. There was this big old potbellied stove in the middle, and the bathrooms were outside. The grades were mixed together. One teacher taught the first and second grades, and another teacher taught the upper ones.

During the Depression, things got bad. My dad passed away when I was about twelve, leaving my mother with eight children and no means of support. There wasn't any welfare. My mother took in washings to make a living, and our job was to pick up the washings on the way home from school. We'd pick up clothes from the schoolteachers, the attorney, and what-have-you. Then, at night, we'd help iron them and fold them. On Saturdays we'd help with the wash, too. We'd put a big old fire out in the patio and a big old tub of water on top of it. Then we'd bring the tub in and wash the clothes.

Summer months would come along and everybody had their chores. My oldest brother always went out and worked, delivering papers, things like that. Two of my sisters did the housework. My next oldest brother and I used to fill up the coal bin for the winter months. We'd go down to the pits where the coal cars would come out. They'd come out loaded full, and some of the coals would fall off. So during the hours when the cars weren't working, we'd go with the other kids from town and fill up our sacks with the coal from the tracks. It took a long time, because that coal bin would hold about three tons of coal. I used to carry a good fifty-pound sack on my back.

When I was a teenager, the Depression began to take a turn. Franklin Roosevelt was elected, and the works projects started. The boys and young men who'd been laid off at the mines went to the CCC camps, and the girls joined the NYA.* When school was over, we'd go and work right there in the school building. We'd help out in the office, do filing and other things. Actually, we didn't do much work—it was our first job. But we learned a lot. It was good experience.

They paid us about twenty-one dollars a month. Out of that we got five and the other sixteen was directly issued to our parents. The same was true of the boys working in the camps. They got about thirty dollars a month. They were allowed to keep five of it. The rest was sent to their families. All of us were hired according to our family income. If a man with a lot of children was unemployed, he was given preference over someone who had less children. They also had projects for women who were widows. They made quilts and mattresses. Those programs were great. Everybody got a chance to work. I think there should be more training programs like that, instead of giveaway programs like welfare.

In my senior year I quit high school to get married. We didn't get along very well, though, and after a stormy couple of years,

* CCC = Civilian Conservation Corps. NYA = National Youth Administration.

I got a divorce. We'd had one child, a son, Carlos. I took Carlos with me and moved to Raton. In Raton I got my first job, working as a salesgirl at eight dollars a week. We used to start to work at seven in the morning and close down at six or seven at night. Then, on days when the miners got paid, they'd make us open up the store again in the evening. They had some type of labor laws in those days, but they weren't made to enforce them. I didn't stay in Raton long, though. My mom had moved to Santa Fe, so I came down here to be with her. She took care of Carlos for me. I got a job at J. C. Penney's, the five-and-ten. I earned about eighteen dollars a week. That was big money. I finished high school, once I got to Santa Fe, too. And then when I was twenty-one, I got married again, and we had two more children.

I was still working at Penney's and even with both our salaries, the two of us were having a hard time supporting the three kids. Then one day a friend asked me, "How much are you earning?" When I told her, she said, "Good grief, you could do better than that on deliveries. They pay twenty-five dollars apiece." That was my introduction to midwifery. Then I met this woman who was a *partera*. She trained me. She'd had many years of experience in midwifery, but she didn't know English. I would go on the deliveries with her and help her out. Then I would type up the birth certificates in English. I also got my LPN by correspondence while I was training with her.* After I'd been with her for about two and a half years, I began building up my own clientele.

I grew up in the days when having babies was a big secret. Nature was a big secret and sex and things like that were taboo. So I never saw a baby being born until I trained to be a midwife.

In the old days, most of my patients were Spanish or Black. We didn't have a county hospital then, and many of them had to have their babies at home for financial reasons. It was a wonderful experience for me. Say, you'd go in on a cold winter morning, and you'd be received in this homey-like atmosphere, a coal or wood stove going nice and warm in the kitchen, with pots and pans of green or red *chile* on top, and some neighbor lady making *tortillas*. The Spanish ladies would prepare themselves weeks in

* LPN = Licensed Practical Nurse certificate.

advance with *empanaditas, bischochitos,* or what-have-you, because the midwife was coming. The midwife was a friend of the family. She made herself that way. We knew when the husbands were unemployed, and we had a lot of deliveries that we were never paid for. Or sometimes people would give us a string of *chile* or they'd butcher a calf for us. That was money. But there we'd be, money or not. The children would be sent off to grandma's or a neighbor's, all excited because they knew when they came home there'd be a new baby—they didn't know where he'd come from, though—and the husbands would be there to help. The Black husbands might participate right there by the bedside. The Spanish husbands would help by keeping the fires up and things like that. In those days, women were never prepared, though. They didn't know anything about their breathing exercises. Nothing. I don't know why the prenatal clinics did not prepare them and teach them more.

Even in those early days I would talk to the people about how important it was for the husband to be there. How important it was for the woman to have this moral support. And I'd encourage the woman. I'd talk to her, tell her what was happening, and try to help her with her breathing.

It's easier today, because the women are better prepared. They've had the breathing exercises and we can work together. Say a woman is three or four hours into her labor and she's just had a contraction. "All right now," I'll tell her. "Now you've had a contraction. Now, relax. When your contraction begins again, take a deep breath, a cleansing breath." And I can tell by what's happening in the vulva or the abdomen when the contraction is coming. The abdomen begins to get hard. That's when I have to get her attention, because it gets to where she doesn't know what she's doing. Just as she goes into delivery, I say "Okay now, pant, pant, pant," just as the head is coming through. "Okay now, pant and then blow. One, two, three, four, blow." And I do it right along with her. So I'm really a coach also. I'm not just delivering, I'm a coach.

Immediately following the delivery, I center myself on that baby's breathing. As soon as the head comes out, even if the body's still in, I start suctioning the mucus and the albumen out of the nostrils and throat. Sometimes things happen so fast between the head and the body that you have to wait until the baby's out completely. Then you suction out the mucus and cut the cord.

After I've delivered the baby, I clean the bed and clean the mother and get her comfortable. Then I take the baby over to a table where there's a light and I recut and retie the cord if it wasn't a neat job the first time, and I put the silver nitrate in his eyes and clean him up, too.

Today most of my patients are *Anglo.* They've taken the LaMaze and LeBoyer classes, and they want to have their babies at home, with their husbands helping them and their friends around.* We're coming out of the hippie life-style now, but I've delivered in houses where everybody was high on something. And I've done deliveries where they were having a religious ceremony right while the baby was being born. That's fine with me. I'm there for one thing—to make sure that the mother and baby are fine. That's all I'm there for.

I won't deliver first babies, though. If a woman is having her first baby, I'll tell her to go to the hospital. There's no sense taking chances. In the old days we didn't have a county hospital. Women didn't have that choice. Now they do. Most of the women I deliver have gone to high school and many of them are college graduates. They've taken all the classes. They've read all the books and still they come here wanting me to do a home delivery for the first birth. I say to them "Look, honey, this is your first baby, your first pregnancy. Go to a doctor. Be in a hospital. You don't even know what a delivery is." And I tell them all the dangers. "Having your baby's not like reading it out of a book, honey. You read a book and you think this is it. No, it isn't. Think about making *tortillas.* You can read about making *tortillas* from a recipe and you most likely will be able to make the dough. But to roll them? And to cook them? You can't learn that from a recipe and you can't learn about deliveries that way, either."

* *LaMaze* = A French obstetrician who developed childbirth exercises for use among working-class women who could not expect to have anesthesia. *LeBoyer* = A French obstetrician who developed a set of theories on the value of a pleasant, tension-free childbirth atmosphere.

To me, a good midwife is someone who's had children of her own at home. It should not be someone who's just looking for a way to make a living. You can't look at midwifery in terms of dollar signs. You have to be sympathetic. You have to also have experienced a little poverty to be a midwife, because a lot of people really don't have the money to go to a hospital. You have to be able to walk in a home and not look at a woman in a bed in labor and say, "Oof! She's got a dirty bed. She's contaminating everything." If you see a mattess on the floor with a sheet that hasn't been changed, you have to know what to do.

I don't think a man should be a midwife, either. If he wants to practice deliveries that bad, let him go on and get his education and become an obstetrician or something. What does he know about having a baby? He'll never experience that pain, even if he is a doctor.

Delivering a baby is not just a business. It's a personal thing, a very personal thing. It's a woman-to-woman relationship

# TWO: THE SOUL OF THE HOME

*La mujer es
el alma
de la casa.*

The woman is
the soul
of the home.

Hispanas born in the 1920s and 1930s worked outside their homes in large numbers; but, like the watchful grandmother at left, most continued to regard care of their families as a first priority. Ida Gutiérrez, right, mother of two young adults, extends nurturance beyond home into her work at the Los Padillas Senior Citizens' Center. Overleaf, she pauses in the background for a photograph with Center visitors.

The New Mexican Hispanas pictured here have managed
to work their way slowly to better-paying, more
prestigious positions than the majority of their
generation. At left, politician Emma Gonzales; at right, a
deputy member of the New Mexico State Labor and
Industrial Commission. Staying on top of a demanding
job while satisfying high standards for family
life is not easy; and these women agree that success
requires the cooperation of other family members.

THE HISPANAS WE INTERVIEWED in the age group from forty-five to sixty years spoke urgently of their work, their homes, and their children. The majority of these women are working at salaried jobs, many while still rearing families. Although they have moved into the public working world, they have not lost their sense of the primacy of their family obligations.

Most of these women were born in rural New Mexican villages during the 1920s and 1930s. Like their foremothers, they were raised in traditional Catholic families, in which the church as well as Hispanic custom and culture were strong forces. Their parents spoke Spanish, and while some women mentioned being taught English at home, most had learned it in school.

As they grew older, these women found the traditional pattern of Hispanic life sharply changed by the Depression and the Second World War. During the Depression many Hispanic farmers were unable to continue supporting themselves in the rural towns where their families had lived for generations. Leaving their homes, some became migrant farm workers. Others went to the city in search of paying jobs. "Those years were really rough," said one woman we interviewed. "There was just no money. Whole families picked up and left their farms, but there weren't many jobs in the city, either." The advent of the war increased urban job opportunities and further stimulated the move from country to town and city. More than 75 percent of the Hispanas whom we interviewed from this generation are urban women.

Despite the poverty of the Depression years, half of the women we spoke with had been able to graduate from high school; one woman had also completed college. Whether they had attended high school or not, all of these women had begun working at paid jobs during their early teens. "We worked in the afternoons after school and on weekends. Often Woolworth's was our training ground." Other women reported working in restaurants and laundries or in *Anglo* houses as maids. Here the pay was low and the hours were long. A small percentage (25 percent) who had learned typing and office skills in high school found jobs as secretaries and file clerks.

Having ventured outside their homes to find jobs at an early age, many of the women found that their parents allowed them more freedom in their social lives than their mothers had known. Several of the women went to California during the Second World War to work in factories and offices. There they lived with relatives, thus making a small detour in the path that had traditionally led from fathers' to husbands' homes.

By the time they were eighteen years old, most of the women had married, leaving work a year or two later to begin their families. Although in the later years of their marriages many of these Hispanas adopted birth control, the heavy prohibitions of the church had earlier discouraged them from such practices. Thus, the majority of the women we interviewed in this generation have borne at least five children. Many of them feel, like their mothers, that a woman's place is in the home. However, because of economic need, most of the women returned to paid employment after their children were born. Those who could afford to, put off looking for outside work until the youngest child started school.

With little or no vocational training, these mothers were once again forced into low-paying jobs, such as waitressing, factory work, and house cleaning. Today, a few of them have worked their way up to white-collar positions through on-the-job experience and volunteer work. Although these jobs may be less strenuous physically than such jobs as house cleaning, the pay is still very low. Two of the women we interviewed have professional jobs; but for most, the combination of family responsibilities, long hours, low pay, and inadequate advancement opportunities has defeated such possibilities.

As urban women who have spent many years working outside their homes, most of the Hispanas in this chapter have led lives quite different from the women of earlier generations. Many feel, nonetheless, that their values are still close to those of their mothers and grandmothers. "Our lives may be different," mused one woman, who is forty-seven, "but for most of us, our feelings, our ideas, they're still the same. Deep down inside we're not the generation that changed. We're the generation that's seen the change."

# Emma Gonzales

Emma Gonzales received us in her office in downtown Albuquerque, making us comfortable with a cup of coffee. On her desk were photographs of her three grandchildren. Now in her fifties, Emma Gonzales has been actively involved in politics for almost twenty years. She has run twice for the position of Bernalillo County clerk and won—thus serving for four years as the only woman in an elective, paid position in the county. She is currently deputy clerk of Bernalillo County.

WHEN I WAS A LITTLE GIRL, my grandmother, my mother's mother, used to tell us stories about the family. She used to tell me about her grandmother's childhood—that would have been in Sandoval County, in the early 1800s. Grandmother said that in those days the Texas cowboys, the *tejanos*, as they used to call them, would come into the Territory [now New Mexico] and take the women and even little girls from their homes and some-times rape them. So when the families knew there was going to be a raid on the village, they would take the girls and hide them in the hills.

My father came to New Mexico from Colorado. He was from an aristocratic family—his mother had come directly from Spain, and the family was financially well off. My mother and father were married when she was sixteen and he was thirty-three years old. Of course, at that time many marriages were pre-arranged. Anyway, he married my mother when she was sixteen and, in a way, he sort of raised her. All her life she was very much under his wing, very sheltered. She never worked outside the home. She never drank alcoholic beverages. She never went to dances, or even knew how to dance. The only place my father ever took her was to the grocery store or to visit relatives.

My father worked for forty-five years as a carpenter for the Santa Fe Railroad shops. We lived near the railroad yard, close to downtown Albuquerque—this was before World War II, and it was very rural. Our family was a close one. There were five chil-dren, and we all grew up very sheltered. My sisters and I were never allowed to do boys' chores. We weren't allowed to have, or even ride, bicycles. And I never went anywhere alone. Every morning we all walked to church. Then, after Mass, we went to school. Sundays were really something great for us, because on Sundays we went to the movies. It only cost ten cents. My dad would give us each a quarter. We would see the movie, buy an ice-cream cone or popcorn, and walk home.

We were all brought up speaking Spanish. We learned English in school. I was probably in junior high when I started really liking languages. I did very well in my Spanish classes. I liked it so much that I decided when I grew up I was going to be a Spanish translator. However, our parents didn't really urge us to go on to college or even to finish high school. Somehow, it just didn't seem that important at that time, particularly for a woman, but I always had this urge to further myself.

All the time that we were growing up, my parents had been very strict with my sisters and myself. We weren't allowed to date or go to dances. The only places were the movies on Sundays in the daytime, or to the nearby skating rink. That's where I met my husband, when we were both fourteen. He was a good skater, and I used to like to watch him skate. His father had died when he was around five years old, and his family of six was having a hard time making it. So when he was fourteen and a half, he enlisted in the army so that he could send his mother an allotment. He lied about his age, but he was big and husky, and they believed him. He served out his two years and was honorably discharged at the age of sixteen and a half. We got married at seventeen, and neither one of us had graduated from high school yet. Most of our friends were married young in those days. It wasn't unusual.

After our marriage, we lived in a small house behind my parents' home. My husband went to school under the G.I. Bill, and I finished high school during that summer.* We had our first child when we were eighteen. Fifteen months after our daughter was born, we had a son.

I did not work away from home while my children were little. I used to take courses at the university at night, but during the day I stayed home and took care of my children. I was really bored, and I begged my husband to let me work, but at first he objected. He was from the old school, and he felt that a woman's place was

---

* *G.I. Bill* = A popular term referring to "government issue" of funds for the education of military veterans.

at home. I didn't really need money—my husband had a job working for a subcontractor. But I really wanted to get out of the house. So I started working very gradually, part-time, so that we could have a little extra money for Christmas. My first job was with American Furniture, working in the toy department during the Christmas rush. After that, they asked me back every now and then when they were busy. So gradually I got started working more and more. Then we started building our own home. My husband was building it all by himself, and we needed to furnish it. It just made sense for me to keep working at the furniture store so that we could get it furnished at a discount.

Our house was built down in the valley, on property given to us by his mother. My husband's mother had land that had been deeded to her grandfather by the King of Spain.* Her family also owned a lot of land where Kirtland Air Force Base is now located, and some in the Manzano Base area—this land also was deeded to their grandfather by the King of Spain. However, the government said they needed this land to build the base, and they condemned it. My husband's uncle hired attorneys and tried everything to keep their land, but they lost out. They were offered less than a hundred thousand dollars for the land. Now that land is priceless.

When the children were four and five years old, I started working full-time. Our mothers took care of our children until they were old enough for kindergarten. By now, my husband didn't object to my working. I was still working at American Furniture as a salesperson, and I got a good commission, but I didn't think it was enough. I'd had good grades in school, and A's in typing and shorthand. So I went to apply for an office job at American Car and Foundry, now the GE plant. I took the test and passed it. I got hired in the personnel department. ACF paid well, and I worked there for approximately six years. From there I applied for another job at Sandia Laboratories and was hired.

---

* Early New Mexican Hispanic communities were established on grants of land from the kings of Spain. After the United States annexed New Mexico (1848) and established new laws, many of these grants were lost, or sold for prices far below their value to speculators, cattle barons, and the National Forest Service. During the Depression of the 1930s, an additional 8,000 acres were lost by Hispanic farmers unable to pay property taxes. See Marc Simmons, *New Mexico: A Bicentennial History* (New York: W. W. Norton & Co., Inc., 1977).

I got active in politics when we moved up to the Heights in 1960. Our nextdoor neighbor, a city judge now, got my husband and me involved in political campaigns. We did a lot of volunteer work for other candidates, but I never thought I would run for office myself.

Those were really busy times. But I had a lot of help. The children were assigned their duties around the house, and by that time my husband helped out too. Of course, he had started doing things around the house while we were still living in the valley. Back then, he used to get home before I did and he would start the dinner. He resented it, but nonetheless he did it. Well, to my husband a meal just isn't a meal without *tortillas*. And they have to be homemade, not store-bought. So I made up cards for him with the recipes for *tortillas*, potato soup, et cetera, and he would fix the meals. He will never forget one time in our valley home, he was mixing the dough and rolling out the *tortillas*. After about a half an hour, he looked up and there were these cousins of his, really *machos*, looking at him through the window. He was embarrassed that they caught him doing that. He got teased about it.

Now, it doesn't bother him in the least. He still gets home before I do and he gets the meals started. As a matter of fact, that's why I'm still working, because he's helped. You see, in a way I'm "liberated," but in another way I still feel my family comes first. It's not worth it to sacrifice the happiness of your husband and your family for your job.

I would probably still be at Sandia today if it hadn't been for a big layoff there in 1972. I had worked up to a grade-35 position and had then taken a university correspondence course, paid for by Sandia, which qualified me for an administrative position as a traffic analyst. But I opted for a voluntary layoff. I knew I could come back any time and do secretarial work.

In 1974 the party was looking for someone to run for county clerk. Traditionally, that's always been a woman's job. I had remained active in politics, and I thought it would be a challenge. I ran for county clerk and won.

But being the county clerk is a hard job. I didn't know how hard it was until I took office. Nonetheless, I learned the job and really enjoyed it. In essence, the clerk is a recorder. All legal documents transacted in Bernalillo County must be recorded and filed in this office. This includes marriage licenses, business licenses, liquor licenses, mortgages, deeds, leases, affidavits, financing agreements, only to mention a few. The clerk oversees the work of sometimes up to sixty people. Then on election day the clerk ministers to over two thousand election officials. She's responsible for all county and state elections. It's a tough job.

I ran again for county clerk in 1976 and won. In 1978 I ran for the office of secretary of state, as I felt I was thoroughly qualified for that position, and I could not run again for the office of county clerk. The law only allows a person to run for two two-year terms. I lost the state election, as I did not have the time needed to campaign. Trying to run for any office when you're the county clerk is a conflict. You're already working twelve-hour days on the election, and then you're supposed to campaign at night and on weekends. It's very strenuous mentally and physically. The county clerk runs the elections and also counts the votes.

Still, it's the only elective woman's paid position we have in the county. Again, I hate to say it's traditional, but it is. And that's really a shame, because I think a woman could do a better job than many of the department heads that are managing the county right now. In the clerk's position, you're budgeted through the County Commission, and you can only do so much. You can't set county policy. Your hands are tied in many areas, but once again, for a woman, it's one of the best jobs available. I hope that in the future more women run for positions not traditionally held by women.

Thinking over what's happened to our generation, my generation, of Hispanic women, in some ways it seems we had a harder time, getting out of the house, than our daughters have, but in some ways we had it easier, too. It was harder for us because few had done it before, and we were breaking tradition. We had to train our spouses and employers to accept us as true career persons and not just working wives. We had it easier in one respect, however, that we had our mothers to take care of our children. Now most mothers and daughters work, making it impossible for the children to have that loving family care of their grandmothers.

When I think of what the future may have in store for me, an old Spanish proverb comes to mind: "Try to reach for the stars, but in the meantime, accomplish what you can."

# Kathy Alarid

We first met Kathy Alarid at the Albuquerque International Women's Year Conference. She moved from one small group of people to another, embracing old friends, smiling at new ones. "Sometimes I feel I've met everyone in Albuquerque," she said. "I've lived here all my life and what with working in the church, the PTA, the Brown Berets, and other Chicano groups, I must have at least one friend in every community group."

Kathy Alarid's experience of life in her fifty years has been diverse, and in many ways she personifies the changes that Hispanas of her generation have seen and felt. Married when she was seventeen, Kathy Alarid reared eleven children. The five youngest are still living with her. For twenty years she worked at home, a traditional housewife. Today she is divorced and working full-time at *Ayuda*, a community service program. Here she talks about the gradual changes that have led to her present life.

I GREW UP AS AN ONLY CHILD. My parents were divorced when I was a baby, and my mother married my stepfather when I was six. So I grew up in several places. I spent some time with my grandfather, some time with my grandmother, and other times with aunts and uncles, but I never really belonged anywhere.

Since I never had a home, I went to a bunch of different schools, sort of shuffled all over the place. After a while they put me in Harwood Girl's School. It was a Methodist boarding school here in town. I was a Catholic—I still am—but that didn't seem to make much difference. We were taught by missionaries and many of them tried to help me. I was a willful, stubborn child.

Then, when I was thirteen, I met Frankie, my husband. I fell in love with him right away. He was my first boyfriend, my first love, and I loved him like I'll never love another man.

Frankie was a year older than I was and he'd already quit school when I met him. He was kind of like an idol to me because he had a job and he was the first one in the neighborhood to get a car. He used to have all his suits custom-made because his family had money. They had a bar and a grocery store.

One day, after about a year, he fell in love with me and we started going around together. For me, that was just it. We went around together all the time after that.

When I was in the ninth grade, I quit Harwood and I started going to Albuquerque High. Then I quit that too, and got a job working in a curio shop. I was fifteen. I worked there for about two years.

Frankie and I were dating quite a lot. We were always together. It seemed we just couldn't leave each other alone. We were so much in love.

When I was sixteen, I got pregnant. Frankie and I got married. I was the happiest girl in the whole world. The two of us came to live with his family and I became like a *chinche,* a bed bug. I clung to his mother, his grandmother, his aunts, and they liked me a whole lot. They still do, even though we're divorced. I guess they liked me so much because I was such an apt pupil. I wanted to learn how to wash and iron, to sew and cook. And I did. I can sew. I can knit. I can crochet. I can embroider. I'm an excellent cook. I made all my baby clothes, and when my kids got married, I made their wedding clothes too.

In the early years, Frankie always had a good job, and I was always at home. I was pregnant fourteen times. Three of my babies died, and so I had eleven children. I got into the marriage but like nobody you've ever seen. It was so neat when the kids came home from school. I'd be cooking, the house always smelled of cookies or cakes or stuff. "Where's my mom?" Joseph would call. He's the oldest. Or I'd be lying in the bedroom nursing the new baby. "Where's my mom?"—that was just the neatest feeling for me.

All of my kids went to Saint John's school; and Frankie's mother had kids who were going there too. She turned me on to the PTA. I would go with her and help out selling bingo and working on the church bazaar, stuff like that. Bit by bit, I got really involved in the school and the church. I was president of the PTA year after year.

Frankie really loved the kids and he was really supportive with them. He used to play with them all the time, and he'd go to the school meetings with me. Our marriage, our family—it was good.

We're divorced now, and I won't ever marry again. I couldn't bring a man into this house or have him over my children. I couldn't do that to my children. I couldn't do that to the man. I couldn't do that to me—because I'll never love anybody like I loved Frankie.

We had been married about sixteen years and he started drinking. Well, he always drank. He was a basketball player, a good basketball player, but always after the games, the drinking. I didn't know what was happening, and neither did he. Gradually, I started going to the meetings at school and the church by myself. He would stay here and I would go. People would say, "Where's Frankie?" I'd say, "Well, he went to another meeting." And then you start the lying because you don't want people to know you're having problems. The kids were growing up, and the drinking got progressively worse. He missed a lot of work. Out of necessity, I had to become both father and mother.

Frankie would work some, and there would be enough money coming in to maintain the family. The older kids were working by then too. They'd give me the three dollars they got from raking leaves to buy bread and toilet paper, but it got to be really lean, even with his family helping out.

To supplement our income, I used to baby-sit for women on welfare, and I used to drive women to pick up their commodities. Before I knew it, I was driving to get my own commodities, because our income was so low we were eligible for the commodities, too. I began to do housework, and I also worked as a maid at the American Bank from five to ten at night.

Finally Frankie got into Alcoholics Anonymous; and it saved his life. It was through the AA that I learned his drinking wasn't my fault. I'd gone through the whole guilt trip, but there I learned it wasn't me. We're contributing factors, but we're not the cause. I learned that Frankie had to do whatever he was going to do on his own. If it was doing away with himself, being found dead in an alley, or sobering up, he had to do it himself. I had to learn to let go, because they can't use us as crutches, and that's what I'd been. Frankie's been on AA for five years now and he hasn't touched a drop. He's been through a whole AA program. He's an advocate of it, and he gives talks all over the state.

But during the time he drank, we just grew apart. I'm talking about a span of ten years now. I became strong. I'd had it in me, but it hadn't come out, because, before, nothing was done without Frankie. He's *macho*. He's Mexican to the core. And strong, a very strong man. Now, though, I began getting strong.

At about this time, I got out of the PTA and the church and I went into social action. I just got into all sorts of community groups because of talking or speaking at meetings or at gatherings. I was on the advisory board of Head Start. I was on the board of directors of Model Cities. I worked as a volunteer with drug addicts and ex-cons.

Then Frankie sobered up one day and he wanted me to stop. He looked at me like he'd been asleep for ten years and then he woke up—and I wasn't the Kathy who said, "Well, if you don't want to go to the Mexican movie, I won't go. If you don't want to go to the picnic, I won't go." I was saying, "I'm going," and I wasn't asking permission. People would call me up on the phone asking about the meeting or the carnival and he would say, "You're not going," and I'd say, "I am."

That was about the time I got my job. I'd been doing volunteer work with a group called *Ayuda*. We had a grant from the state and we operated two hot lines for minority people. We gave information on what to do about runaway kids, girls getting pregnant, boys overdosing, Social Security, disability information. We were like a counseling service. That's when I met Dick, the guy from the welfare program. He'd seen me working at *Ayuda* and he said, "Kathy, we need you down here at welfare. We want to hire you. You don't need to type. You don't need to file. I just want you to be at the desk so when someone comes in here with a problem and they're not eligible for welfare, you let them walk out with a good feeling. You try to tell them where they can find help." I said, "I don't know if I can do it." I'd never been out of my home that much and I thought my kids needed me. He said, "You go home and you talk to your kids." So I came home, and I told the kids, and Joseph said to me, "Mom, if you don't take that job, I'll never speak to you again." So I took the job, and that's what I've been doing for the past five years, and I really enjoy it.

By now, living together was really intolerable for Frankie and me. I realized it. He realized it. Then one day, I just had to make a decision. It was like that movie, *The Way We Were*, because that's what happened. We still loved each other, but . . . We'd start in talking about unions. He'd start telling me that Chicanos have high-up positions at GE, and I'd tell him, "Name them on one hand." He'd say, "I don't want to talk to you because you're crazy." I'd say, "Well, you're stupid." It was just no good once we lost that respect for each other.

After the divorce, nobody swamped me with offers to take me out, except younger men. See, a Mexican man, a traditional Mexican male, does not like the type of woman that I am now. To the Chicanos my age, I'm an abomination. I talk too much. I'm too smart. I'm too strong.

The guy that I've been going with for the past three years is eighteen years younger than I am. He's a Puerto Rican from New York. I met him when he was going to college out here. I had never really been attracted to younger men, but Raul has taught me many things that I didn't know. I know that I have taught him, too. I've taught him tolerance and I've taught him patience.

If somebody would have told me three years ago that I'd be going through a trip like this, I'd have said, "You're crazy." Today, I'm often on TV and radio programs, talking about what the Chicana has to go through to be herself. First, she's got to go through the man. You find any Chicana that's into something, that's an activist, she's divorced.

# Esperanza Salcido

Esperanza Salcido and her husband, Joe, live in Albuquerque in the house they built while their children were growing up, twenty-two years ago. At fifty-six, Esperanza Salcido has always planned her life around her family. Her children are grown now, but her work of caring for others has changed very little. Today she looks after her young grandchildren. "Recently my dad got sick," she said, "so I'm taking care of him, too. He lives all alone. He's almost blind and can't leave the house. Yes, it's hard sometimes, but that's what families are all about."

ALL OF MY FAMILY comes from the northern part of the state, from Dawson and from Cimarron. Dawson's a ghost town today, but when we were growing up it was a big coal-mining center. There were two or three thousand people living there. My father worked in the boiler room at the coal mine. That was a good job, and even though there were six of us kids, our family was pretty comfortable for a while.

When I was in the seventh grade, we moved to a ranch near Cimarron. I really enjoyed that. I was a tomboy, and I used to take care of the field with my brother. We'd go out and chop wood, bring it in, and saw it. I like that work a lot. You know, I can't say I really wished I was a boy, but I'll never forget when I first found out that my bust was growing. I was so disappointed. I went into my mother's sewing supplies and got me some of mother's ticking and I tied this double piece of ticking all around me. I made it so tight, I could hardly breathe. I was so afraid those little balls would show through my shirt. I tried to hide them as long as I could. It was actually about three or four days until my mother found out. She told me they were going to show whether I liked it or not. A little bit later, our home economics teacher talked to us all about our periods, and I realized that I just had to learn to be a lady. So I started wearing dresses, and kind of settled down.

My sister and I went to a small high school in town. This was during the Depression. There was just no money, and mothers who lived out on the ranch had no way to dress their kids for school or get cars to come into town. Our mother never even came to town but once a month to buy the groceries. The only way for us children to get to town was by school bus. And, this was a nice thing about that small school, every year each teacher would take a girl from one of the ranches as a daughter—one teacher took my older sister and me. She took us to mother-and-daughter banquets, and she took us to teas and things that our mother couldn't do because she had no transportation and no money.

When I graduated from high school, I was the valedictorian of the class and I got a couple of scholarships for college—one to Lubbock, Texas, and the other to Highlands in Las Vegas.* I guess if I'd have pushed it and not been a pansy, I could have gone, but there was just no money, and I couldn't see leaving my family and going to some distant town. So I stayed at home, and I worked for about a year as a waitress and a typist. Then I got married.

I met Joe while we were still in high school, and he was the first person that I'd really dated. My parents used to let me go out but they were real strict. I had to be home by nine-thirty. So I didn't date much until I was sixteen or seventeen, and that's when I started going out with Jocy. We dated each other all through high school. Our parents couldn't afford to give us a wedding, so we saved up our money for a year and paid for our own.

I was so green when I got married. I didn't know anything. I didn't know about sex, and I didn't know about birth control either. Of course, Joe was a little more educated than I was, and he really took care of me. You know, they say that at sixteen or seventeen most girls know how to make love. Well, I didn't. This is something that I've never said to anybody, but my husband's the one that taught me—I guess that's why we learned to love each other and understand each other so well, because what I know, he taught me.

All the time that Joe and I were dating, we'd talked about our family and our house. We were going to have the perfect kids. We never wanted a large family, though. We both came from large families, and I could remember how my mother made out order forms from the catalogue each year. First, she'd tell us all to sit down and write what we'd like to have. Well, with six children, her order would be 'way too big by the time it was completed,

* Now New Mexico Highlands University.

and I could just see the pain in her eyes, having to scratch through the stuff she thought we didn't need. I knew I never wanted to go through that when I got married.

In those days, though, you just didn't let the world know you were practicing birth control. We weren't real religious, but of course we were Catholics, and it wasn't your best friend that told you anything like this. When we'd been married about a year, Donna was born. We were living on the farm with Joe's family at the time, and it was Joseph's mother, Grandma Lina, she took me right under her wing. She knew I didn't want a large family, and she told me I should make Joseph take care of me. So he did. Then, a few years later, when we moved to town, the wife of the president of the Downtown Merchant's Bank helped me out. She was an educated woman. She knew all about birth control, and she wrote down a list of what I could use and what I could get. Then we went into the drug store. It took me all afternoon to look for the stuff. She'd watch the door. When she saw somebody coming that we knew, she'd say, "Here comes somebody," and I'd drop everything. It was worth it, though. Now we have just the three children, two girls and a boy, and only one of them a surprise.

To Joseph and me, our kids and our home have always been very important. I never really wanted to work outside the house, and Joe had a good paying job, so we decided I would stay home while the kids were little, because they needed me. Once Teresa was in first grade, I worked as a caterer while we built our house. Since we always paid cash, it took us a long time.

Then I came home when the kids were teenagers because those can be difficult years, especially for a boy. That time, I stayed home ten years. I went back to work when Teresa was ready for college, and I worked until she was through school. Now I'm home again, taking care of Teresa's kids while she teaches.

You know, we thought we'd planned everything just right, but as I look back on it, even with all our planning, the kids missed out on some things when I went to work. I think that's one of the reasons that our youngest never learned Spanish. Now, the older two picked it up from their grandpaents, but we'd moved to Albuquerque by the time Teresa was born. And then, once I got to working, I just didn't stop to think about it.

You know how those little things can go to pot when a mother's not at home. A couple of years elapsed, and when we all of a sudden woke up, Teresa didn't know a word of Spanish. And now my grandchildren don't speak it either. I've even gone so far as to buy those Spanish records—but they're just stone cold to it.

Actually, Joe and I have had a pretty wonderful life together. We've raised three kids, and I'd say we've given them a pretty good home. I've always liked housework, and I've always taken pride in my house. I really like doing the wash and seeing my clean floors. But my husband has always helped me. We've been married thirty-five years and I can honestly say he's done the dishes all the time. He used to bathe the kids too. When I was working, we even shared the ironing, until the kids were old enough to do their own. Then everybody ironed—the girls and the boys both. We've always helped each other out on everything. But then, we're really a close family.

To me, that closeness is one of the strengths of the Spanish family. It's not just the mother and the father, but the grandmother, the aunts, and the uncles. Up until last year when my mother passed away, we'd all get together at Christmas, Easter, Thanksgiving. Grandma, grandpa, all the kids and the grandchildren, and we had a ball. We just wouldn't feel it was a holiday if we couldn't get together.

I like to call that closeness "family unity." And it's something I've worked for every day. When my kids were growing up, we would have a big dinner every night, and there was always a centerpiece at my table. Each of the children had their little chores to get ready for dinner, and we never sat down without saying grace. Everyone always had something to say, and someone would usually say too much. But to me, that was the important time. It was the only time of the day when all of us could be together. It was the height of my day to have my family sit at that table. I used to work all day long for just that one hour.

# Ida Gutiérrez

Although with Ida Gutiérrez's silvering hair and her fifty-four years she might by now be a grandmother, she explains, "I got married kind of old, and I still have to wait for my heart's desire, *los nietos* (grandchildren)."

As a young woman, Ida Gutiérrez left New Mexico to work in California, returning in her late twenties to her birthplace, the village of Los Padillas. There she married and started a small farm on her family's property. Five years ago, her husband died. Ida Gutiérrez lives on the farm now with her seventeen-year-old son, walking each morning to her work at the community center, which used to be her elementary school.

We spent five months getting acquainted with Ida Gutiérrez before she would talk with us formally, "with that tape recorder on." When at last she had told us her story, she listened carefully to the taped conversation and then asked us for a copy, so that she could make a gift of it to her daughter.

WHEN I WAS YOUNG, TIMES WERE BAD. Back in those days, you know, we didn't used to have regular jobs, nobody. We lived on a farm and it seemed our parents were always working. You see, we depended upon our farming, our crops, because there was no money coming in from anywhere. There were no jobs at all. My dad used to raise corn, a lot of corn and wheat. He'd harvest the corn and he'd grind it. He'd send the wheat off to be turned into flour.

With some of the corn my mother made *chicos* (dried corn). She'd soak the corn ears in their husks and then she'd put them in the *horno* (outdoor adobe oven) to smoke. When they were done, she'd take them out, bend back the husks, and hang them on the wall to dry. Then she'd just boil them up with the beans or whatever we were having for dinner.

My dad raised sheep too. He'd raise them, and when they were about two years old, he'd butcher them. I used to help him with the *matanza* (slaughter). We used to use every bit of that sheep, every bit except for the feet and the tail. We'd take the head and skin it and put it in the oven to bake. When it was done, we took it out and broke it, then we ate the brains. They were real good. Just thinking about it makes me hungry.

We didn't have refrigerators or ice boxes then, so when we had plenty of meat, my mom would cut it in slices, very thin, very, very thin, salt it, and put it on wires to dry outside where she hung the clothes. After the meat was dry she would get a big stone and go over and over it with the stone, rubbing it to make it tender.

At the end of every summer my mother would can the fruits and the vegetables for the next year. She had this extra wood stove that she put outside because it got so hot. She'd build up a big hot fire, and then she'd take the corn, the *chiles,* the peaches, and the tomatoes and she'd put them in jars and boil them in a big kettle. My sister and I, we used to help her. But *hijo!* that was hard work! My mother would can from morning to evening—one week, two weeks, however long it took. Sometimes two women would come together and help each other, to make it easier. They'd let the housework go and just can until they were done—because if they didn't do that, then how in the world were we going to eat?

We used to go to the *fiestas,* lots of *fiestas.* We had our church over here in Los Padillas and our patron saint was San Andrés. We used to celebrate that day. We used to go to church and my mother used to make all kinds of goodies. Then, we had a small hall where we went to dance. We'd invite people to come over, and we'd feed them, and go dancing in the afternoon. We used to make a big deal of it—buy a new dress and get all fixed up for that day, because it was something real special for us. We used to have other *fiestas* too. When me and my brother made our first Holy Communion, my mother had a special party for us afterward and invited all our relatives. She made *chile rellenos* (stuffed chile peppers) and *sopa.* I'll never forget it.

Of course, we had to go to school, too, but I never liked school that much. When I first started, I didn't speak any English. None of us did. I was about six or seven years old. Anyhow, they taught us our ABC's and how to speak English—all that. It wasn't too bad. But then later I got sick, and I missed a lot of school. After that it was hard to keep up, so I just went up to the ninth grade, and then I went to work.

I got my first job when I was sixteen, working in town—Albuquerque—at the El Fidel Hotel. I used to go on the bus and then, after a while, my sister and I moved in to stay with my uncle. He had a little apartment there.

I started out cleaning rooms. Then I got promoted to elevator operator. I made fifty cents an hour, and I had it made. That was about three dollars a day, and it wasn't too hard—not like cleaning rooms. Just once in a while sort of boring, going up and down all day. A lot of other Spanish people worked there, and some Black people too. No Indians though, or *Anglos*. The *Anglos* had nicer jobs, as salesladies and things like that.

After about three years, I moved out to California. It was during the war, and there were a lot of jobs. My brother got a good job out there and my dad said I could move out there and stay with him and his wife. In California, I worked as a packer in a milk carton factory. California pays good. I remember getting fifty dollars a week! At that time, that was a lot of money. A lot of money. They had a union, too. That was nice because they paid sick leave and vacation. I used to come see my folks every vacation, because I lived out there for five years.

But then my mother got sick, so I moved back here to take care of her, and I worked at McClellan's, Woolworth's. I was a saleslady. I sold yardsticks and curtain rods.

I had a lot of fun when I was single. I loved to dance—I'd always wanted to be a dancer. I liked to dance the cha-chas, the mambos, the rhumbas—all that. I started going to the dances at about sixteen, and I had a lot of, not exactly boyfriends, but friends, you know, dancers. But I didn't care to get too serious with anyone, because I was having so much fun as a single. To tell you the truth, I didn't get serious until I was about twenty-six. And I just saw this boy all of a sudden and I liked him. I met him at a dance. I had come home from California, like I said, and when I came back to the farm, I was so sophisticated. I thought I was *it*. I had real beautiful clothes and everything. Well, I went to the dance and there he was. He had just been out in San Francisco. He was real handsome. He was all dressed up real nice, and he was a real good dancer—so that's how we got together.

I'd never brought anybody home before, because my dad was kind of strict, and he said somebody had to be real special before we brought him home. Well, when I got serious with my husband, I did bring him home, and my dad questioned him—where he came from, and this and that. He liked him. He said, "He's a good worker, you can tell."

We had a small wedding at my parents' home, real small. I didn't care to have a big wedding since I liked him so much. I guess when you love a person you don't care for them to spend that much money on a wedding, because you figure you'll get to use that money later—which we did.

After I got married, though, he was real strict. I used to have these dancing dresses that were real pretty and low cut, but once I got married to him, he made me not wear those dresses any more. No more dancing either—and he was a good dancer himself. I thought he would take me out at least every other weekend. But he didn't. He said, "No more dancing. You danced enough already. You're twenty-six years old. Aren't you tired of dancing? No more!" I really missed it, but I said, "Well, I love him, and it's true I have danced enough already. So I might as well stay home and cook and clean house."

I was used to freedom. Do anything I wanted, wash dishes and clean house when I wanted. Maybe if I didn't want to curl my hair that day, do what I want. It was hard to get used to his ways. They were nice, you know—there's nothing wrong with being neat—but it was hard on me, because I was single for a long time, and then this guy comes into my life telling me to do all these things.

I guess the beginning was the best part, though. I think at the beginning you have more attention from your husband, and more love. Afterwards it wears out a little bit, and he wasn't the type that would tell you, "I love you." He wasn't *mieloso* (mushy). He used to say, "Why, I married you, and you know that I love you. I don't have to be telling you every little while I love you. I love you, I bring you the things you need, and I married you."

He was a good provider. When we were just married, he said to me, "Anything that you need, you come to me. I'll give you some money." I used to tell him, "I don't want your money. I have to work to get my own." He said, "But you're married now. You're working right here at home." But to me—having his money, spending it and then telling him, "I paid this for that, and this for that," and showing him all the receipts! Where this dime went, where that dime went! Sometimes I didn't know, and it would drive me crazy. *Híjola!* But at the same time, you give in if you love the guy. And then sometimes you say to yourself, "Why, I don't want to be by myself all my life, so I'm going to try." You know what I mean?

We were married for about nine years before my kids were born, and I was worried I might not have too much time for having kids, because once you change life, you don't have any. So I talked to the Lord and I said, "Look, Lord, you give me a little girl the first. I want a boy and a girl—but first of all, you give me the girl right away 'cause I might be too old for both." Sure enough, I had my first one when I was thirty-five, and she was a girl. I was very happy. I think a daughter is always closer to a mother. They have the same things in common. Then, three years later, my boy was born. I had a boy and a girl. I think that was enough.

All while my kids were growing up I stayed home with them and cooked and cleaned house. Five years ago, my husband died and I went back to work part-time. You see, my boy is only seventeen. That's why I work part-time. I have to stay home on account of my son. If I don't stay home, he won't like to stay home either, and he might take off or something. So I have my responsibilities—I have to stay home and see what happens for his future, make sure he finishes high school. My two kids are my pride and joy, and when they both have their education, I'll know I've done my obligation.

I had a hard time finding a job when I went back to work. For a while, I worked in a *tortilla* factory over here, Bueno's. That was a hard job. Somebody would make the dough and other people would feed it into the machine to make the *tortillas*. The *tortillas* would come down the belt and you'd just grab them by twelve and put them in a sack. And, eeeye, when I just started, that belt moved so fast. You should have seen the pile of *tortillas!* They jammed that belt, and there I was—buried in *tortillas*. After I got the practice, it was not so bad. But at first, there were *tortillas* all over.

I only worked at Bueno's for a little while, though. Then I started working as a maid, and I'll tell you, this housework, it's the hardest of them all. It's not a regular job, you know. You work only one day with each people. It's not like when you're working one job. If you don't work, you don't get paid. You don't get vacations or sick leave. They pay you two dollars, one seventy-five, or two thirty an hour. Some of the ladies pay Social Security, but some of them don't. It all depends. If you're lucky, you find a woman that is real nice to you. If you get to meet one of those ladies, you got it made—they pay for your gas, or they give you bus money. But not all people are the same. I've worked for rich ladies who thought'd they'd go broke if they gave me a Coca-Cola. And they make you work real hard for your money, too— clean the walls, get down on your knees and scrub the floor.

All the women I've worked for are *Anglos*. I guess the Spanish people, they just do it themselves.

It was while I was doing housework that I got my job over here, working with the seniors. I used to work two or three days a week cleaning houses. Then on my days off, I'd go over to the community center and talk to the seniors over there and help out. I volunteered because I have always liked people and I feel compassion toward the elderly and the sick. And Mr. Herman Joffit, he's head of the seniors' program, offered me a job. He'd seen me there several times, and then one day he called at the house and he said, "Ida, I've seen the way you treat the people over there. How would you like to work for the seniors?" And I said, "Well, I'm not experienced. What would I do?" And he said, "The same work you're doing now. Talk to the people and help them with their meals." That was three years ago, and I've been working here ever since.

You know, a long time ago, women, poor things, they didn't let them step a step out of the house. They couldn't do anything but stay home and cook beans and *chile* and make *tortillas*. That's about all. But nowadays, most of my friends have jobs. Most women have jobs.

Everything's different. Like my own daughter, she's very different from me. She's much more classy—is that the word? She's much more sophisticated. I guess it's because she has her education. I didn't have that—I only finished the eighth grade. But my own daughter, she can stand up and speak for herself real good.

She knows everything, almost, about everything. Anyone who talks to her thinks she's around twenty-two. She is so mature. Even myself, when I talk to her and joke, I feel a little out of it because she's very mature. She even has her own car. She's too much in advance. Really.

Still, I think it's nice for a woman to know everything. Women today have studied hard, and if they're capable enough to do it—why not? What's the difference between a woman and a man? You know what? It would be nice if a woman ran for president.

# Margaret Torres

Margaret Torres, small and brisk, walked quickly from her office to our interview in the lunchroom of the State Office Building. At forty-seven, she is an equal employment officer for the New Mexico State Employment Division, and the mother of six children. For eight years, she has worked full-time while caring for her family. Recently her husband died, leaving Margaret Torres to carry on these responsibilities alone.

Margaret Torres enjoys her work. Over the years in which she has moved from a clerical job to an administrative one, she has encountered many of the problems that women face in being supervised and supervising others. She feels that her problems at work, however, have been less difficult than the private strain of watching her children grow up in ways that are "different, different from my life."

I HAVE A HARD TIME thinking of myself as an individual. It seems I've always been a daughter, a wife, or a mother. I've always been working and raising children.

I came from a family of nine kids, and when we were growing up, each of us had our responsibilities. We had to help iron, hang out our clothes, chop wood for the wood stove. We had a house in downtown Albuquerque with a big old tree in the front yard, and I used to climb that tree all the time. I was a real tomboy. I used to play marbles with my brother every day. Then sometimes the whole family would get together and play games, see who could name all the capitals of the states, things like that. Having the whole family together was really nice.

When I was growing up, we didn't speak just Spanish in my house. My mother and father spoke both Spanish and English, and my dad always encouraged our English. As a matter of fact, I spoke English so well that when I went to school they put me right into second grade.

I went to Albuquerque High School, and I used to work at Woolworth's after school and on weekends. I knew I'd have to get a full-time job as soon as I finished high school. I'd taken the full commercial course, and my typing teacher got me a job the week before I graduated, working for an insurance company. My first boss was really something. Whenever he wrote a letter, he'd make it one long sentence, like a paragraph. I thought it was dumb just having one sentence, so I used to break it up. Well, one

time he told me, "You know, you don't think like a Spanish person, the way you correct my English." I said, "Well, I am Spanish," and he said, "I know, but I'll let you correct my letters.
Only, don't tell anybody else, because I let you do it only because
you don't think like a Spanish person." And you know what? He
was Spanish himself.

Around the same time, I met my husband. He was a ware-
houseman and he worked for Sandia Corporation. We dated each
other for about three years, and then, when I was twenty-one, we
got married. We wanted to start our family right away, so I quit
my job and stayed home to have my babies.

Frank and I wanted four children, but when we were having
our babies, it was very different from now. I knew about birth
control when I got married, but the Catholic Church taught us
that it was bad. It was wrong. It was a sin. When I had my third
baby, the doctor said to me, "You are too little to be having so
many babies. You should have a Cesarean and have your tubes
tied up." So I told my husband, and we went to see the priest that
married us. "Oh, no, you shouldn't," *me dice* (he said). "You
should trust in the Lord and everything will be all right." Well,
that time it was. She was five weeks early and she was small. But
I had three more after that, with complications every time. Six
kids, such a burden to my husband. It's hard on the woman
having them, but the biggest responsibility is the financial one,
and the man always feels that.

Anyway, several years after I'd had the kids and was taking
classes in theology, this new priest came. He told us to think for
ourselves. He said, "You don't have to have a big family and
bring your standard of living 'way down." After I started hearing
this, I said, "No more, the heck with this noise," but by then it
was too late. Our priest had just been doing what he thought was
right, but I sure wish I'd realized that sooner. Of course, now I
wouldn't trade my last two for anything. They're all I have with
me now. This Janet, she's got a real personality. She's my buddy
every weekend.

We always wanted for our kids to have their education. We
encouraged them to make good grades, and we never let them
work too much after school because we figured a good education
would pay off better in the long run. As I said, we didn't plan to
have six. We planned to have four, and we wanted to be able to

send them all to college. When they were little, I used to type at home, but when Manuel was in high school, my husband said to me, "If you'll go to work so that we can help out Manuel and the others that want to go to college, I promise I'll make supper for you every day, and I'll help you with the house." So I did, and Manuel went to college. Then the two oldest girls didn't want to go, but Suzanna, the third girl, is up at Highlands University in Las Vegas, and Frankie and Janet are doing real well in school here.

When I went back to work, I started out for the state as a secretary, and now I've worked myself up to an equal employment officer, handling the office with the largest workload.

After I had been working for about a year my husband seemed a little bit resentful, but I told him, "Anytime you want me to quit, I quit." That changed that. As I progressed and got my promotions, he was always very pleased, and always encouraged me. Last year I had to do a training program for all the secretaries in our division. I hadn't been asked to do it until the night before. I came home and told my husband, "I'm going to conduct a training program and have to stay overnight in Santa Fe with my secretary." "Great," he said. "Okay," I told him, "now, you need to help me." And he did. We sat down and I asked him, "When you walk into an office, what do you notice the most, telephone etiquette, things like that?" He was very enthusiastic about the whole project and helped me figure out a format for my presentation.

So I didn't have much problem with him. I did run into resentment with men at work, though. Right now I'm head of my office. I have one man working for me and two secretaries. My big boss is a man and he has always been very encouraging, suggesting that I take the state test necessary for promotion. He's the one that said, "Margaret, you're going to run this office." But there's another man in my office that is older than I. He's been in the labor field longer than I have, and he felt that he should be the supervisor even though my boss didn't seem to think so and I had passed my test with a good score. It has been very hard for him to accept the fact that I am his supervisor. I don't think he has ever admitted it, even to himself. He complained quite a bit, until finally one day I had all that I could take, so I went to his office, and I just sat down and I talked to him.

"Look," I said, "you knew what you were going to get when you came here." Well, he calmed down after I talked to him a bit, and things are okay now.

So I'm very fortunate in my office. I have seen cases in other offices, though, where a man can be the biggest goof-off there is, and he'll still get more money just because he's a man, even when the woman has the more responsible job. Like when I was a secretary for that insurance company—toward the end, I was doing all the work but my boss got all the credit.

I still remember that, and it is one thing that I try not to do with my own secretary, Gracie. She's been with me for four years. She's real good, and I try not to make things too hard on her. Now I've gotten to where I just write out my own letters rather than give dictation because that just takes her more time. But sometimes I see the other deputy putting a lot of work on her, and I'll tell him, "We shouldn't have to put Gracie through all that. You go through your files and *you* decide which ones you want to set up for a hearing, instead of having her do it."

Now we're getting another investigator, another man, and I told Gracie, "When he comes in, we're going to tell him about filing and show him how to use the Xerox machine. We're not going to have any more of this stuff, Gracie. He does things on his own." If we can do things on our own, there's no reason why everybody else can't. Just because they're wearing trousers, they shouldn't throw it on someone else. But I guess it's because I've been through it myself that I'm not going to do something like that to another woman.

I love my job. I like dealing with people, helping them. I love it. I would never be able to have a job where I couldn't see the public—I'd just wilt. Sometimes it gets rough when we have really bad days with several hearings, but I feel very fortunate that when my husband died, last May, I was already established here in my job. Otherwise, I'd have been lost.

It was rough, anyway. He had been sick for the last two years, and he'd had quite a few surgeries. I'm not going to say our marriage was made in heaven. We'd had our difficult years, too. Any marriage does. But he was a good husband to me and he was a great father to his kids.

Any time we had problems with the kids, we could talk things over. I didn't have to make those decisions alone. Raising kids *cuando está sola* (when you're alone), that's really difficult.

I have two daughters with children, now. My oldest daughter, Barbara, is very square, or as Suzanna says, "Mom, she's just like you. She's very Catholic." But my other daughter, my daughter Helen, she's nineteen and she has a beautiful little girl, and she keeps telling me she'll get married, but she's not. It's just something I have to accept. I fought it at first. I was hurt when she first got pregnant, and I asked her, "Well? Are you going to get married?" She said, "Eventually," but they didn't.

Anyway, she said, "eventually"—when's that? I've tried to talk to her, and before he died, my husband used to talk to the boy, but it didn't help.

I've tried not to push it because my older son told me the more I push, the more they'll wait, but every so often I just can't keep quiet. And last summer, we built a patio in the yard, and I said to them, "You could get married in the patio. You could have just a small wedding, just the family. Don't wait until I die," I told them. "Don't wait until I die or Grandma or Grandpa dies," but they just looked at me.

And I love my daughter and I love my granddaughter and the father is a very good boy. They've been together since right after she got pregnant. They have an apartment two blocks away, and anything I need, they'll do for me, but they say they just don't feel it's time. Well, I don't know when it's going to be the right time. I do everything I can to help them, but I don't accept it. I can't. I can't accept it. I just can't.

I've seen couples, like my secretary's sister. She lived with this fellow for four years before they got married, but they didn't have any children. If there weren't a child, I'd say that's something else.

Oh, well, I wouldn't like it anyway. Not my daughter. Your daughters are special. Your daughters are pure. I guess it's because it's my own child; that's why it's hard.

But, anyway, this is the thing that is different. Different from my life.

# THREE: LITTLE BY LITTLE

*Poco
a poco
se anda
lejos.*

Little
by little
you walk
a long
way.

Hispanas who grew up in the 1940s and 1950s began to move forward in education. In far greater numbers than their mothers, they completed high school. A fortunate, hard-working few entered colleges; some, like the librarian at left, went on to graduate school. Patricia Luna, right, who experienced the bitterness of racial discrimination in her own student days, now counsels students at the University of New Mexico.

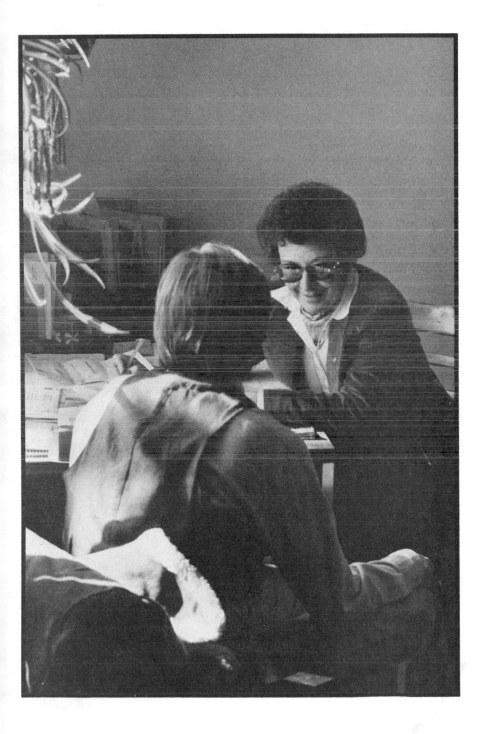

Eloisa Gallegos, left, instructs her daughter in house-
painting techniques. She has reared her four
children and five sisters and brothers on her own,
supporting them with skilled work as a house painter,
supplemented by domestic work. At right, Jennie
Montoya finds time for thoughtful attention to her two
young children. Her busy life includes companionship
with her husband and other family members, work
as a writer and a graduate student, and service to social
causes. Freed of traditional restrictions on Hispanic
women, accustomed to urban life, fluent in English,
women such as these can fend for themselves confidently
in an *Anglo* world, as their foremothers could not.
They have walked a long way; but they have not left
behind their devotion to families and community.

THE HISPANAS IN THEIR EARLY THIRTIES to their mid-forties are women of the same generation as the compilers of this book, with whom we could directly compare notes on the changing patterns of growing up female in the 1940s and 1950s.

The women we interviewed in this age group were primarily urban, living now in Albuquerque. Like the generation of women before them, they were born in the country and moved to the city as teenagers or young adults. As children, many had spoken Spanish at home. However, some had also been taught English by their parents, and a few had been reared speaking only English. "My parents never spoke Spanish to me while I was growing up. They spoke it to my grandparents and to each other, but they didn't want me to speak it. They were afraid I'd have an accent in English and that would make it hard for me in school or when I went to get a job."

Concerned about their daughters' educations, parents who could afford to often sent them to Catholic schools. "The nuns were really strict," recalled Ana Gerimini, "and I guess they taught me a lot of things really well. On the other hand, it was also a very narrow experience. We never learned about Plato or Spinoza or any of those philosophers who weren't Catholic."

High school was accompanied by part-time jobs. "We all worked," said Delia Vigil. "That was the only way we could afford to go to school." Picking cotton, waiting tables, cleaning houses, and baby-sitting, some women helped their families by paying for part of their room and board. Others used their money to buy lunches, school clothes, and occasional party dresses. "We all saved up our money for prom dresses. Then, each of us bought one dress and we traded around for every dance," one of the women recalled.

Most of the women of this generation had full-time jobs by the time they were nineteen. "Our parents always taught us that once we got out of high school, we were supposed to get a job. They didn't expect us to go to college, but they wanted us to be able to support ourselves and our families if we had to, or at least be able to help out our kids. As a matter of fact, that was supposed to be the real point of working, so that our kids' lives could be better than ours and our parents' had been."

After they had worked for a few years, a number of the women we interviewed in this age group did go on to college, in most cases by working their way through, winning scholarships, or both. However, these college-educated women see themselves as atypical of their generation. As Ana Gerimini pointed out, "Most Chicanas from my generation simply have not had these opportunities. Today many of us are still struggling to make ends meet."

The majority of these women married between the ages of eighteen and twenty-two, and began to have children soon after that. By this time, the Hispanic community's attitude toward birth control had become somewhat more liberal, and birth control information had also become more generally available. Many of the women returned to work soon after their children were born. A very few continued to stay at home after their children reached school age.

The women who have spent a great deal of time working and studying outside their homes often view their jobs not simply as a means of survival or of providing advantages for their children, but also as meaningful careers. "I tried to stay home after my second daughter was born, but it was awful. I really missed my work. I missed being out in the world." While a number of these career women are divorced, several of those who are married reported that their husbands do "help out" in caring for the children and the house.

As a group, these women have had much more direct contact with *Anglo* society than had the older Hispanas we interviewed. Some women spoke of their private hurt and anger at encountering racial discrimination in school or on the job, while others described their feelings of powerlessness, faced with an urban society's indifference to the people of the *barrio*. "You know, the people down here, they're poor, but to me they're special, and it really makes me angry when the city comes in and just tears our neighborhood apart. Last year they ripped up two blocks of houses to put in temporary school buildings when there were empty lots they could have used. And now they're getting ready to build an overpass down the street, and they're going to tear down that old building with that big mural of Our Lady of Guadalupe on the front. It's hard for the people who live down here to fight back. You're so busy working. You're so busy trying to feed your family."

Many who spoke especially strongly about economic and social problems had gone to college and now feel a responsibility to use their education in ways that will help other Hispanics. "After my children are in school," said Jennie Montoya, "I would either like to go to law school or get my Ph.D. in English. Whatever is going to be more important to our people."

Whether in college, working for wages, or working at home, the socially conscious women of this generation often see their concerns as extensions of the attitudes they learned from their mothers. "My own mother stayed at home all the time," said a thirty-eight-year-old teacher's aid. "As far as she was concerned, her home life was it. Now, I try to be as good a wife and as good a mother as possible, but I still need to do something out there. I still want to make my community a better place. But, you know, part of that comes from my mother. '*Ayúdale a la gente* (Help the people),' she used to say. She didn't leave her home, but if someone came to her in need of help, *o un plato de comida* (or a plate of food), she wouldn't turn them down. She stressed that so much. I'm just the same, but I go out. I take part in the schools, the committees, the associations. I want to help not just the neighbors, but the whole community."

# Patricia Luna

Patricia Luna is especially concerned with Third World people and
with women. When we first met her, she was a counselor at the
Women's Center at the University of New Mexico. Now working in the
University's Office of School Relations, she spends a large portion
of her time counseling women students and helping them to define
their needs and their goals. In addition to her full-time job, Patricia
Luna conducts frequent workshops on racial awareness. In 1977 she
was one of the New Mexico delegates to the International Women's
Year Conference in Houston, Texas.*

I WAS BORN IN SOUTHERN NEW MEXICO in a little farming town
of about two hundred people. During World War I, my parents
moved to San Francisco. And that's where I went to first grade.
Because I didn't know any English, I was put in a class with re-
tarded kids. I grew so despondent that my parents sent me back
to New Mexico to live with my grandparents in the village where
I was born, and I went to school there in a four-room schoolhouse.
There were about fifty kids in the whole school, and almost all
of them Chicano. So were the teachers. In fact, most of the teachers spoke Spanish. So it wasn't until I was in high school that I
heard people say, "No, don't speak Spanish." If you were caught
speaking Spanish in my high school, even in the hallways, there
was harassment.

My high school years were sort of difficult. By then my parents
had moved back to our village. I used to live with them for part
of the time and my grandparents for the other part. Now, my
grandfather and my father were very different. My grandfather
always spoke to me as a strong person, capable of doing just about
anything. My grandfather was a farmer, and when I lived on the
farm with him and with my uncles, I used to do everything they

* Held in Houston, November 18–21, 1977, the conference was sponsored by
the United States Commission on the Observance of International Women's
Year and attended by women representatives from every state in the nation.
Meeting together, they drew up a broad program calling for social, economic,
and political reforms, later issued in *The Spirit of Houston, The First National
Women's Conference: An Official Report to the President, the Congress and
the People of the United States, March 1978.*

did, work in the fields, whatever. If there was something I didn't know how to do, they wouldn't do it for me, they'd teach me.

My father, on the other hand, would say, "Oh, you don't know how to do this or that or the other." It made me feel like maybe I wasn't supposed to know how to do these things. He wanted me to take home ec. Gad, I hated home ec. I wanted to take industrial arts. I liked the smell of wood, I liked creating things. I'd watched my grandfather mix *adobes*, I knew all that stuff. But I couldn't take industrial arts. I had to take home ec.

So all during my teenage years I had these two influences, one that kind of showed me my way was okay and the other that said, "But it isn't okay."

I'm not really sure what made me decide to go to college. I remember my male principal told me I didn't have the brains or the skills I needed to go. But then I had a woman teacher who said, "You can be anything you want to be," and my grandfather said, "You can do anything you want to do." So one day I talked to a recruiter. Then I went home and I said, "I'm going to college." I really can't remember if they said anything to me about it, one way or the other. I'm sure in a way they had a sense of pride about it and felt good about it. But they never said, "We're really happy that you made this choice."

I think my experiences in college were probably the most shattering. That's where I ran into blatant racism. My friends who were darker than I really were discriminated against. Some were among the brighter students, and they'd make A's on tests and get C's in courses. There used to be signs on lawns, "Apartment for Rent—No Mexicans or Dogs." During those years my sense of outrage kept growing and growing. For a long time I felt there must be something wrong with me. There must be something wrong with us. Slowly, I started to feel, "Hell *no*, there isn't anything wrong with us. Something's wrong with a world that won't accept people." But those were shattering experiences.

I dated a lot in college. I went out with a variety of men, both *Anglo* and Chicano. But I never really wanted to get married and raise a family. A lot of Chicanas feel that's the role of the woman. It's her religious duty to have children. The pressure is really very heavy, but I never felt that way. I don't think I would be a good mother. There are people who can be good mothers and people who can't. I think it's important to recognize that not everyone has a mothering instinct. I like kids if I can have them for an hour and then they go off. For a while I got some pressure from my folks. They used to make subtle remarks about "when we have grandchildren." It's not because I told them I'm not going to get married. I just decided not to discuss it. And I like being single. You know, the longer you're single, the better it feels. That sense of independence—it feels good.

In the Office of School Relations I do recruiting and I work with returning women students. I also do women's workshops. I work a lot with the issues of racism and feminism.

Sometimes it's very hard to explain racism in New Mexico. It can be very subtle. It's not always blatant. We've never had the Ku Klux Klan here, so to speak, but we've had other forms of oppression, like not being able to speak your own language in school, like not being hired for certain jobs. But it's hard to make that connection. Partly because of our religious upbringing, our people have always wanted to say that we're above that and turn the other cheek, but you can't keep ignoring it forever. Sometimes in workshops, Chicanas will say, "Well, I've never felt a feeling of racism"—and yet their children or their grandchildren can't speak Spanish.

Often *Anglo* women get defensive. They like to think that all women have similar problems because we're women. Well, Rosa Parks was not kicked off that bus in Alabama because she was a woman. She was kicked off because she was a Black woman. And that's the difference. Unless you can feel the situation that she was in, you can't possibly sensitize yourself to the fact that there is a difference between being a minority woman and being a woman.

I've done workshops on this campus a number of times about minority women. The *Anglo* women don't show up because they feel it's not their issue. To be a feminist or a human being is to learn about all people! If you're a feminist, how in the hell are you going to know minority women if you don't even know what their needs are? Reading a book about them isn't going to help you. You have to hear about these issues from people who are feeling them if you ever expect to become sensitized.

When I first heard of the International Women's Year Confer-

ence I thought, "Oh yeah, another women's meeting. All the
middle-class *Anglo* women will sit down to discuss all the problems. Once again they'll ignore minority women. Period."
That's all I thought. Then I saw the tentative schedule for the
state IWY convention.* There were workshops on the problems
of rural women, the problems of urban women, the problems
of international women. There was nothing on Hispanic women,
nothing on Black women. "That's interesting," I thought. "I
wonder why?" So I called up the organizers. I couldn't get a response. I tried to go to several meetings, but they weren't held in
the scheduled places. Finally, I wrote a letter. No response. At
that point I got fed up and I thought, "I'll just not bother." But a
friend of mine called up and said, "Come on. We can't let them
do that to us." And I said, "You're right." So one afternoon
we got together a whole bunch of Chicanas. We decided if we
couldn't get a minority women's workshop, we were going to
put together a Chicana slate. We were going to nominate our own
representatives and draw up our own resolutions. By that time,
the national IWY organization had sent out a list of tentative
resolutions. There were proposals for battered women, proposals
for older women, this, that, and the other. They were pretty
lengthy. Then I saw the minority women's proposal. It was all
of ten lines, and I was angry. I remember one *Anglo* woman said
to me, "I don't know why you're so upset. Chicana women have
a lot of liberties in this state, and they occupy a lot of positions in
high government." At that I got really angry, because I knew she
was wrong. "Where?" I said. "Just show me where!"

That was during the time that we were writing out our slate,
and the other women at the meeting asked me to run. "Why
not?" I said. So we put together our slate and a package of resolutions for Chicanas. Then we rented a room at the inn next door
to the conference, and we invited all the Hispanic women at
the conference to come to that room and debate the resolutions
because we wanted them to be representative of what other
Chicanas in Albuquerque felt also. We had close to a hundred
women in that room. Some of them were older, some of them

* The Houston IWY conference was preceded by state conferences at which
platforms were adopted and delegates to the November meeting were chosen.

were rural, and they all spoke about their different needs. How we need federal funding for translators in medical agencies and welfare agencies so that the older people who speak only Spanish will know what's going on. Issues like that.

One of the most infuriating things at the state conference was that our workshop was not considered legal. The only minority women's workshop that was legal was the one for Native American women because it had been officially scheduled. So we asked them if we could present our resolutions and our slate at their workshop because we couldn't get them in anywhere else, and they said we could.

So we put our resolutions through and then we presented them and our slate to the whole state conference. Several of the *Anglo* women asked me, "How do you Chicanas stand on abortion?" And I said, "Well, we've had a long talk about that among those of us who are on the delegate slate, and we've decided that although many of us don't like the idea of abortion because it goes against our religion, other women may need that right. It has to remain an open option. Actually, though, for minority women, the problem is not so much abortion but sterilization." Then we had the elections and I won. I was chosen as one of the delegates to go to Houston.

Over the next few months some of us from the New Mexico delegation got in touch with other Chicanas all over the country so that by the time we arrived at the national convention we could have our act together. Once we got to Houston, the Hispanic women's caucus got together and discussed our priorities. Then we met with the other women in the minority women's coalition and we put all our resolutions and our ideas together.

The most thrilling time at the convention was the voting session when all of the delegates came together to vote on the conference resolutions. First of all, it was very moving to see such a powerful woman as Coretta King speaking for Black women. Then, after the minority resolutions were read, all the minority women stood up to second the minority resolutions. That was just incredible because, you know, when we all stood up we were a majority!

I'm not sure that any of the resolutions that came out of Houston are going to be worked on by the Congress. I think it's mainly symbolic. Nationally, there aren't going to be too many things that change. But for minority women—for Hispanic women— it was important for two reasons. First, because Hispanic women and other minorities came out of the woodwork and said, "We're not going to take a lousy ten- or eleven-line paragraph in your national plan of action. You've been telling us what's important to us all along. We're not going to let you do that any more. We're going to decide what's important to us." And we did. We argued and disagreed, but when we were out there on that floor, we were united. Secondly, for a long time minority male organizations have supported each other verbally, but they have never really come together, never really united. We women were able to do that. We were able to do what the men have never been able to do, get together and stand up for ourselves and each other.

You know, often people speak of Chicanas as being passive. Well, we're not. If we were passive, how could we raise our families? Passivity does not lead to good motherhood. But we haven't really been able to express ourselves before—because in the Chicano movement, we were relegated to the kitchen, while in the women's movement we were told our problems were no different from the problems of all women. We haven't really had a voice. But now we are saying that we're not going to take a back seat any longer. Either give us a voice or we're going to speak anyway. We will work in the feminist movement, but only if we can keep our cultural feelings, our needs and ideals intact. We are going to be in charge of our own destiny. If feminists will not accept this, we will unite outside of the feminist movement. We will keep our unique identity.

# Ana Gerimini

Ana Gerimini, thirty-seven, has spent her adult life going to school, working as a full-time teacher, and raising three children with her husband, Michael.

"I do what I can," she says, "and I try not to worry about the rest of it. It's an attitude the old Mexicans used to have. They were farmers, and they could till the earth and plant the seeds, but if it didn't rain the crops wouldn't come, and *que podemos hacer*, what can we do about it? That's the way I look at things."

Three years ago Ana Gerimini stopped teaching to accept a fellowship in a full-time Ph.D. program. Here, she muses about her education, taking stock of what she's learned—both in and out of school.

I WAS BORN ON A FARM, just east of Lucero, in a little *adobe* house that my mother and my older brother and sisters built. I was the youngest one of nine children, and I was really raised by my sisters. We were always together, playing or doing chores. We had to haul water, feed the chickens and the pigs. In the summertime we had to take the cows up to the mountain, to graze and water them.

We didn't have any electricity, so my mom did a lot of canning and drying and smoking. She'd can fruits and vegetables, and she used to boil meat and can it, too.

At night when I was little my dad used to read me fairy tales by the kerosene lamp after he came home from work. He'd read them first in English, then he'd translate them into Spanish so that I could understand because we didn't speak English at home.

When I was eleven my dad lost his job. He was a janitor in the state hospital at Las Vegas and he got fired when the Republicans won, because he was supporting the Democrats. So he moved the whole family up to Cheyenne, Wyoming.

All my life I'd lived in this little town with one main street and two general stores, where everybody knew everybody. Cheyenne was the big city, and things were pretty awful if you happened to be Chicano. The signs in the restaurants said "No Dogs and No Mexicans Allowed," and a lot of kids were afraid to say they were Spanish. That's when I really had to learn English because I spoke it *mocho* (broken). Back in Lucero, we'd had to speak it in the classroom, and they'd told us to speak it on the playground, too, but we never did unless we were playing "gringo"—and even then we spoke it all *mocho.*

In Cheyenne there were only two other Chicano students in my class. There we were—with all these Todds and Hobbs and Smiths and Pomeroys. My own name, Rosario, sounded strange. It was rough on me, but it was worse for my next oldest brother and sister. He was in the ninth grade and she was in the eleventh. They both just dropped out. It was so hard to adjust.

In eighth grade, the next year, I had a really good teacher. She spent a lot of time with me helping me learn the language. The school we went to was a parochial one. Our parents thought we would get a better education there, and maybe we did, but it was very narrow. We never learned about Plato or Spinoza or any of those philosophers who weren't Catholic. Those nuns used to really fill us up with guilt. I remember, in ninth grade, our religion book told us it was a sin to commit "the marriage act." They never told us what "the marriage act" was, though. I waited that whole year to find out.

When I was sixteen, I got my first job. It was a typing job that one of the sisters had found for me because I was such a good typist. I only worked there for a week, then they told me not to come back because I was a Mexican. I never forgot that afternoon when they fired me. I walked and walked, all up and down town, crying because I had no place to go, no one to tell. I never thought about telling my parents. There was nothing they could do about it.

So all through high school, I worked in a motel and in this big cafe, as a bus girl. I didn't think much about going to college. To me the *gringos* were the smart ones. They were the ones in the "in crowd." The ones who always looked great. They were so on top! After graduation, the *gringos* went off to college and I went to work for the State Department of Education. I used to help the bookkeeper and do all kinds of other piddly little jobs. For a while, they had me typing this stupid newsletter for one of the educational consultants. That woman earned a thousand dollars a month, and she used to plagiarize for this newsletter of hers. Well, I started thinking about her plagiarizing and making money and all those other smart-looking *gringos* who had gone on to college, and I thought, "If those people can make it through, I probably can, too."

One of my sisters lived in Las Vegas; so I decided I'd live with her and go to Highlands. My dad wasn't too pleased about my leaving home. I was the baby, and I guess he'd figured I'd stay around for a while. But there wasn't much he could do about it.

Up at Highlands, I got a job in the library. I worked there fifteen hours a week while I was going to school. I majored in Spanish and business education, and then I picked up my teaching hours, too, just in case I couldn't find a job.

While I was at Highlands I met Michael, and we decided to get married. We were married in June of 1964, and I graduated in August. That really disappointed my father. I think he figured that once I'd finished college, I was going to come back home again. Then, too, Michael's being an *italiano* didn't make him too happy. After a while he came around, though.

When I got married I was still pretty programed for a woman's role. My mom hadn't had much education and my father had never helped her around the house, so naturally I thought I should do all the little homey things I'd seen her do. In the beginning, I even got up early to fix Michael's breakfast, but then he told me, "I don't eat breakfast"—so I never did it again. Actually, he's never wanted me to be a housewife. Every time I've stayed home, he's always said to me, "Why don't you go do something?"

That first year, I got a job teaching at the Las Vegas junior high, and Michael went to work for the welfare department. Then I got pregnant, so I had to quit in the spring, because they wouldn't let you work if you were pregnant. Michelle was born in September, and I got a baby-sitter and went back to work in November.

Gina was born in August of '67. That year, I did a lot of substitute teaching because it was kind of late to get a full-time job. Then in '68 I went to work for the Job Corps.

That was an interesting job. They hired me to teach English as a second language because of my background in Spanish. The students there were really tough urban women, teenagers from Chicago and New York. The Job Corps brought them out here

to teach them skills like typing, shorthand, dental technology—
all women-type vocations. The women were pretty neat, but the
program was really ridiculous. Here they expected these kids,
who had about an elementary-level education, to learn all these
skills in a year. It couldn't be done. Now, some of the women who
took courses like electronics did okay. They got good jobs. But
then there were others—like the nurses' aides. I would have
been afraid to have one of those students for a nurse's aide!

While I was at Job Corps I started working on my master's. Job
Corps had this deal where they'd pay 75 percent of your schooling, so I started taking courses, at first for the hell of it. Then, too,
by that time Michael was in school at UNM and I thought that
way we'd both be doing something. Besides, it gave me a night
out. I finished my master's in '72, in reading, and got a job in a
local college prep program for students from poverty backgrounds. That was pretty awful also. Just like the Job Corps, it
seemed built to fail. Neither of those two programs was set up
realistically, with an idea of how to really help students. Instead, their attitude was one of, "We really need federal monies.
How do we get them?" That became the principal issue. They
would push students through English classes without teaching
them the skills, or just pass them on, giving them college credit
for watered-down courses.

I had been thinking for a while about getting my Ph.D., but it
had always been one of those unreachable goals. Then suddenly
the prep program ended, and there I was without a job. I had to
make a decision. There were a number of minority scholarships
available for people who wanted to work in education, but it was
really a hard idea for me to accept. I kept thinking, if I apply for
that federal money, will people think I'm looking for a handout?
Finally, I went ahead and applied anyway, because I thought going to school full-time would be the only way I'd get my Ph.D.
I got the money, and I started going to school. But it took me
almost a full year to get over the feeling I was getting a handout.

Part of the reason I feel that way is because of the way *Anglos*
look at the quota system. It always seems *Anglos* are patroniz-
ing me. They assume that of course I'll get my degree because
I'm a Chicana, and they think professors will make it easier on
me. I guess I've worked in too many special programs, and I've

seen people pushed through just so that the program could show gains.

But it's really important to me to prove to myself that I can get a Ph.D.—because I'm a Chicana, and I think it's important that we go that far and become a model for others who still haven't gotten there. When I get out, I'll probably have better job opportunities, but that's not the real reason. What I really want when I get out is do research in Chicano learning styles, because a lot of the literature that has come out is so superficial. We have to find ways to evaluate school programs in subjects such as bilingual ed. Usually, bilingual ed is dealt with only on an emotional level. You're not allowed to question it. You can talk about how great it is, how nice it is, but you can't discuss which parts of it don't work. And if we don't ask questions like that, I don't know how we're ever going to make it better.

I've been working on my Ph.D. for three years now, and Michael has been really supportive. He helps me with the kids and with the house. The kids have been funny about it, though. They never argued about my teaching. They accepted it because they thought it gave them more money. But I noticed that when I started going back to school and doing my own thing, they made more comments about my not being around. Finally I told them, "You know I get paid for going to school. I'm still bringing money home." That kind of stopped them. But I don't think my getting a doctorate really means anything to them.

On the other hand, I think my folks are really proud of me. They don't say anything directly to me, but my mother will tell my niece that she's glad I'm going to school because I've worked so hard all my life, and now I'm doing something for *me*. They don't bug me as much about coming to see them as they used to. And—like the last time I was up there, I told my mother to wake me to go to church with her early on Sunday morning. Then I stayed up studying until two. The next morning I got up at about ten, and I said to her, "Why didn't you wake me?" and she said, "Well, I saw you stayed up until two." That's all she said, but I know what she meant.

I'm supposed to graduate this December. My parents are really old, but I hope they can come to my graduation. When I got my B.A., after four years of hard work, it kind of felt like a letdown.

Then, when I got my master's, I called up my parents and I said, "Well, I'll go through the line if you're coming down." My mother said, "We don't know if we can make it." Well, I figured nobody would come, so I didn't make a reservation. Then, about a week before, they called up and said, "We're coming to your graduation." I said, "Well, forget it 'cause I'm not going." And I really felt rotten, because that would have been their pleasure. Now I've decided, if they're still alive, if my dad can still travel, when I get my degree, I'll go through the line. I have a hard time just doing it for myself because when I got my B.A., it just wasn't a big thing. But it will be all right if I'm doing it for them. Then it will be a big thing.

# Delia Vigil

*Delia Vigil grew up sharing a close family life with her parents and grandparents, her brother, and her three sisters. Today, at thirty-five, she is trying to preserve some of that closeness for her own children. She and her husband, Jake, who is in the military, have three sons: Manuel, twelve; Daniel, eleven; and Marco, six; and they are expecting another child in December. On the summer morning when we interviewed her, Delia Vigil spoke of the care of her family and her work in the home as the job of "a professional homemaker."*

MY WHOLE FAMILY COMES from a small farming town up north of Las Vegas. By the time we kids came along, though, there wasn't much money in farming. So my dad used to go up to Cheyenne for a year at a time. He'd sheepherd up there in Wyoming while mom took care of the five of us.

It was nice in the country, because we lived right near our grandparents. And if things got boring at home, I'd go over and stay with them. My grandpa had a sawmill. He'd put us to work piling up the bark that came off the logs and sweeping the sawdust away from the machine. My grandma and grandpa lived in a log cabin and they didn't have any electricity. So we used to carry the butter and milk down to the stream. That was our refrigerator. We'd take a string and tie one end around the butter and put the other end under a rock.

We were very poor when we lived on the farm, and we didn't have any real toys. We didn't have that much time to play anyway, because if we weren't helping mom with the chores at home we were helping our grandparents or we were working in the fields. Whether we were working or playing, we were always outside.

Of course, everybody had animals. Once my grandma gave me a duck, and I raised him like a chicken. The dumb thing didn't even know how to swim. Well, one Saturday morning when I was bathed and all dressed up in my best clothes, I decided my duck should learn to swim. I put him in the pool at the back of our house, with a string around his neck. The duck almost drowned a couple of times, but then he got the hang of it and swam 'way out into the middle. So I trotted in after him.

When we came out, I got the beating of my life and the duck ended up in the soup.

When I was about six or seven, we moved to Albuquerque and my dad started driving a truck. We still didn't have much money, though, and my parents could only afford one good school jacket for me and my sister. One day she would wear the jacket to school and I'd wear a sweater. The next day I'd wear the jacket and she'd wear the sweater. It didn't matter how cold it got. That was all there was. You wore two or three sweaters or you wore the jacket, and if there was one good pair of shoes we'd take turns on that, too.

We couldn't afford store-bought bread for our lunches or waxed paper for sandwiches, so my mother would save the wrapping paper from bread when she could afford it and then she would make biscuits and fry up potatoes. That was our lunch. I used to get real irritated with those kids who were a little better off 'cause they were always flashing around their peanut butter and jelly sandwiches. You know how nutritionists are always saying you have to have a well-balanced breakfast, like eggs and cereal and bacon—all that is hogwash. For breakfast we'd have *tortillas* and *chile* and refried beans. Sometimes we'd eat that three times a day. Sometimes we'd only have one meal a day if things were very, very difficult. It sounds hard and it was, but it was real good, too. Coming home after school, I could smell my mother's *tortillas* a block away, and by the time we got to the house she'd have a big old stack of them ready. We'd be munching and she'd be swatting us for getting into what was supper.

My mom and dad always spent a lot of time with us. My dad used to fix breakfast for us. After we moved to town he spent every weekend helping out around the house. He'd wash, he'd clean, anything. He made sure my brother helped out, too. If it was Joe's turn to clean the kitchen, he cleaned it and he scrubbed the floors. When it came time for ironing, we all did our own, even my brother. After our work was done, my dad would take us out in the street to play baseball, or sometimes we'd go over to the neighbor's house and watch TV.

We all worked. That was the only way we could afford to go to school. I got my first job when I was in the seventh or eighth grade. I worked at a drive-in just around the corner from the

house. I'd go to work at about six and come home at about mid-
night. When we weren't working or in school, we spent most of
our time with the family. We'd sit around the table after supper
and we'd listen to the radio. We'd dance and everybody'd try to
learn how to polka. My dad would make a parcheesi board and
we'd play games or build houses out of matchsticks—things
like that.

As we got older, it was a bit crowded. We had a two-bedroom
house. The four girls shared one room with two twin beds, two
sisters in a bed. My brother used the couch out in the living room,
then my parents had the other bedroom. We did some crazy
things. Sometimes my father wouldn't let my sister go out and
they'd have these big fights. He'd shout, "You're not going
out," and he'd send her to bed. After everyone else was asleep,
she'd sneak out the window. She'd push my dad's car out of the
driveway and around the block and take off in it. When she came
back, she'd tap at the window. I'd go out and we'd brush the foot-
prints out of the driveway with branches. Then we'd go back in
the window and go to bed.

When we were in high school our mother used to say all the
time, "Now, remember, you have to get a steady job." Well, I
wanted to be a dancer. Right after graduation I was interviewed
for a job at the Majestic Dance Studio. They hired me as an in-
structor. "Are you crazy?" said my mother. "What kind of a job
is that, running all over the country?" So I didn't take it. I ended
up in an office instead. It was either that or leave home, and it
never occurred to any of us to leave home, not until we got
married.

I got a job as a secretary working for Huntington Electric.
That's where I was working when I met Jake. I met him on a blind
date. He was in the military, and his best buddy was going out
with one of the girls I worked with. She fixed us up. We went out
with each other for about six months and then we decided to get
married.

I quit work just before Manuel was born, and I've been home
ever since. Daniel was born the next year, and then five years
later, just as the two older ones were ready to start school, Marco
came along.

You know, today sometimes I feel like I'm my mother living

her life over again, struggling along from paycheck to paycheck, striving for my kids to get a better education than what we were able to get. I feel if I can just get my kids through high school and keep them emotionally on the right track until they're eighteen or twenty, I'll have accomplished what I set out to do as a home-maker.

There are days now when I'll sit and wonder how my life would have been if I had left home, gotten another job, maybe married someone from another state. How different would it have been? Probably not too much. I'd still have the same basic rules for myself. I would never have married out of the Catholic Church, and I would have worked very hard at finding someone who's Spanish-American. I don't think I would have worked after marriage either. I've never been a believer that a woman has to work, to fulfill her life. For myself, I've always felt that there's more pride and satisfaction in what you can accomplish in your own home. It shows how much intelligence you have, to accomplish miracles, practically, with the little that you've got at home.

I don't have any one real priority for my life. I kind of take each day at a time, because if I have to have a priority, it means I have to plan something, and I don't like to do that because you never know when it's going to change. Like, Marco starts school this September and I was all set to go to sewing classes, bowl in the daytime, and redecorate my whole house. Well, all that's out now—because, frankly, with this new baby we just won't be able to afford it.

I get up in the morning at about seven and before I even leave my room I make my bed. Then I go to make breakfast. I won't let the kids go out of this house without something to eat. I don't care if it's a bologna sandwich. When they decide what they're going to eat, I fix it, cereal, pancakes, whatever. As soon as I get rid of everybody, I sit down, drink my coffee, and work out what I need to do today. Is it going to be the laundry, or am I going to iron? If I'm real energetic, I just might bake something. Then at eleven I have to go and get the kids and feed them lunch. In the afternoon I'll watch TV for an hour or so, or I'll go to the store. Then it's three-thirty and time to start dinner for them. Really it's more like a snack, 'cause they go to Little League practice in the evening, so they eat one half their dinner before they go and the other half when they get back. Jake takes them to practice at six. While they're at practice, that's my time alone. Then I rest mentally.

That's my everyday work. That and the cleaning. I really like to clean. It's a challenge to have a big mess on your hands and in a certain length of time you can vacuum, you can dust and move the furniture so that it looks different. You can wash the windows, and if you even have a tiny bit of spare time, you can do wonders with contact paper. Now I'm not too crazy about cooking and I don't like to iron, but I have a real hangup about cleaning and moving the furniture around. I figure that's where I get my changes. When you're an average family and all you have is your home and what's in it, you have to do the changes yourself. It's not like the woman who can go to Europe for a month or Las Vegas for a week. Hell! I've never even been out of New Mexico. I have to make my own changes right here, myself.

Sometimes this place is just like Grand Central Station. There are times when I'm in p.j.'s, the whole place is in an uproar, I've got two tons of laundry to do—and I'll be damned if an aunt doesn't drop in and we sit there and drink coffee for two hours; and there goes my whole day—shot. Or I'll be in the middle of making *tortillas* and a couple of my girl friends will come by and they'll say, "Hey, let's go to the flea market," or "I want to check out something at the second-hand store," and I'll say, "I can't go. I've got to get this done first." Well, before you know it, one will start rolling them and another will start cooking. We get it done in half the time. Then we take off.

There are always people coming in and out. I like to keep up with my relatives and friends because I think you need that to keep going. With two teenagers around here, this place can get pretty hairy, and I can get real depressed, but then my aunt will come over or my girl friend, and we'll yak or we'll go someplace, and suddenly I don't have a problem any more. They sort of just lift me up.

You know, it used to be real simple when the kids were babies. You fed them. You bathed them. You played with them, and that was that. You didn't have to worry about what they were thinking, what their moods were as now you do. Now when they're ready to talk, you have to be ready to listen, but then they don't always want to talk to you. One day Manuel will look at me and smile—"Ye gad, you're neat, Mom," and the next day there'll be that look on his face of "Oh, are you sickening." He doesn't want to talk to me. He doesn't want to be anywhere near me. Just that look on his face makes me feel really rejected. My husband I can cope with. I can say, "If you don't like it, damn it, get out." I don't want to get mad with the boys, though, because they're going through one hell of a time right now and I don't want them to feel they're monsters. I want to be as understanding as I can so that when they're over these two or three years when it's most trying, they will be at least satisfied that things worked out pretty well considering the pain in the butt they gave us, and I will have the peace of mind that I've done my best.

I stay up a lot at nights thinking how I'm going to react if Manuel or Daniel says this or that. It's very hard. It takes a lot of mental work, and that's why I need the time by myself.

Like last night, when the boys were going to practice, Jake said to me, "Do you want to go?" and I said, "No. Just leave me alone and get these kids the hell out of here. I have a lot of mental work to do." Because the boys and this being pregnant were really getting me down.

Mental work. I guess I do it at least once a month—more now, with the boys at this age. I have to be by myself to begin with, and it sounds like I've probably lost a screw or something, but I talk to myself, sometimes I cry or slam the door. I just have to work all these pressures out of my system, or I'll get sick. I have to analyze my own feelings. Is it really that important that it should bother me so much? Should I say something to Jake or to the boys? Should I try to figure out a way to take a day or two off? Do I really have a good reason to feel sorry for myself? Damn right I do! Then I may cry, or stop and try to be sensible about the whole thing. Then I'll cry again, so that by the time they come back, I'm not wound up any more. I've figured, "Well, hell! this is the way it has to be." But these everyday pressures, they are the worst part of being a homemaker.

That's how I think of myself, as a homemaker, a professional homemaker. I'm not a housewife. To me the word housewife makes you sound like you're baby-sitting your home. I'm a homemaker, and that takes a lot of intelligence, whether people realize it or not. It doesn't take a degree. It's a different type. You really have to work at it. You don't work at it five days a week, eight to five. You work at it twenty-four hours a day, seven days a week, every day of your life—and there aren't too many people who can do that.

I've had a lot of people look at me real shocked because they'll ask me where I'm employed, and I won't say "I'm not." I'll say, "I'm a homemaker, a professional homemaker." And I strongly believe there isn't a man on earth that could afford my services—childbearing, the cooking, the cleaning, the emotional work that you have to do to raise your kids. That's why I hate this women's lib crap, too. There isn't a man that can do this job as professionally as I can. There are other women who can do the job, but I don't feel a man can. He cannot cope with the pressures. To me, this is a woman's instinct

# Eloisa Gallegos

For generations, southwestern Hispanic women have plastered and painted their houses. In earlier days, they mixed sand, earth, and water into a thick paste which they smoothed over the *adobe* brick walls. Then they collected gypsum rock and baked it for three days in an earthen oven until it crumbled into a powder, which they mixed with water and wheat flour to make a whitewash.

Today, Eloisa Gallegos is following in the footsteps of her Hispanic foremothers. A single parent who has raised nine children, she has supported herself and her family for almost twenty years by painting houses in the summer, the spring, and the fall. During the winter, when arthritis prevents her from working outside, she hires out by day as a house cleaner. However, she much prefers painting. "Up in the mountains," she says, "I never heard of men painting their homes. I always thought it was a woman's job."

WHEN I WAS A CHILD UP IN THE MOUNTAINS, my dad used to work in the roads doing construction. There were ten of us kids, and since we were mostly girls, my dad just started us all off doing all kinds of chores, outside and inside. Though, now that I think about it, I guess we did mostly boys' chores. We used to have to go out and work in the fields, picking the pumpkins, peas, and beans. Then, my sister and I, we used to get the truck and go up to the mountains to haul wood. We'd haul it home and my dad would come down to town to sell it during the winter.

My mom did most of the inside work, raising the younger kids and delivering her own babies. We were all born at home, except for the last two. By that time my folks had moved to town, so those two were born in a hospital, but they both died. The rest of us, the ones that she delivered herself, well, we're all alive.

Quite a few people used to tell my dad—this one lady got real mad at him and told him—"Why on earth are you putting your girls to do that job for? They're not boys," and he told them, "Well, they're going to have to learn to work hard, in case they get themselves a bum." He says he didn't see nothing wrong with any one of us working hard. I'm glad he made us work hard because I learned a lot of things, and I don't think nothing of my problems, because I can get out there and solve them one way or another, even if I never have done the job. It doesn't worry me because I know that I can do it. Plumbing, electric work, I get up on the roof and I patch leaks. Or like mechanic work, I had two trucks and I used to fix them all by myself, except for the motors. Starters, alternators, I did that all by myself just by getting in and doing it. I feel like a woman can do anything a man does if she really wants to do it. She'll do it. That is, unless she's ill. Like me during the winter now. I can't help it because I have arthritis, and I just can't move during the winter unless I take maybe six or seven aspirins and I hate to be on aspirins every day. But there's a lot of things a woman can do that a man does. Anyway, that's the way I was raised.

I dropped out of school when I was in the ninth grade, because at that time they only went up to the ninth grade in the mountains, and if I'd continued school, I'd have had to ride the bus down into town. I'd already started working, cleaning houses after school, and painting them, things like that. And my parents really needed the help, so I thought I'd just keep on working. I started working in trade of material things, because people didn't have very much monies. It never really mattered to me what kind of jobs I got, but I guess I liked painting the best. I always thought it was a woman's job. Up in the mountains where we lived, I never heard of men painting their homes.

When I was a teenager my parents were very strict about our going out with guys. They never really talked to us about sex. The only thing they would ever say was, "If you go out with guys, you're going to get pregnant, so don't go out with them at all." My dad would really threaten my life if I went out with them. In those days most parents up in the mountains were like that. Most of the girls in our village got married when they were very, very young. Some were only thirteen or fourteen. So when I was seventeen years old, I saw myself as an old maid. I thought I was never going to get married, just because I saw the whole town getting married at thirteen or fourteen. I already had a boyfriend, but I wasn't allowed to go out with him. So finally I decided to get married. I was seventeen.

We got married not knowing about birth control. I remember telling my neighbors, "I'm going to get married, but I'm not gonna have babies until four years from now." Well, how on earth was that going to happen? I talked like I knew what was going on, but I didn't. I got pregnant right away. I had all four of my kids one right after another, with only one year off in the middle somewhere. About the time the third one was born, I started hearing about birth control. Then after my fourth one, the doctor told me my blood was too weak or something, and I shouldn't have any more. That's when I started using birth control.

All that time, though, I kept right on working and I kept painting. I did housework too, and sometimes I'd go out and do a lot of handyman work. Then I'd clean houses. I was about nineteen when I did housework for this lady who was the nicest one of all. She used to drive my kids to my mother's so my mother could take care of them while I worked. That lady did a lot of things for me.

When my youngest child was a year old, my husband took off. Then my mother died and I had to take responsibility for five other kids. Nine kids! Well, I got some help from the welfare and my sisters and brothers too, and I kept right on painting. But it was really kind of bad when I had them all nine at the same time. I guess I could have made more money, but I was working for myself, and I didn't charge people very much because I never got in contact with people that could afford to pay that much money.

I worked that way for twenty years, painting in the summer and doing housework in the winter. Now I still do housework in the winter. I work for seven different people, a day for each one of them, and I get two dollars and twenty-five cents an hour. According to what I heard, this is the lowest rate even for housework.

You know, it's nice and quiet there while I'm cleaning. I try to get away from the noise at home once in a while. But still, it's the same old housework. You still go do the same old things. And when I go out to clean houses it makes me feel bad because I think, "What am I doing here cleaning a clean house when my house really needs cleaning?" I feel like I do forty dollars of housework. So I don't think it's worth it, going out to do housework for fifteen dollars a day.

This year I started working for Yucca Construction, because

I figured I would have more jobs that way. Raymond and James
pay me three dollars an hour. I know that men painters get a lot
more than that, but I feel I just started working for them, so I
don't mind. I do want them to give me a raise once in a while,
though, and I already told them I expect that.

When I'm painting on my own, the people know beforehand
who I am, and that way I'd never run into discrimination. But
now, working for Raymond and James, it's different. Like last
month, I was working for this elderly lady, and she kept on going
outside all morning long, and she kept talking to me about different things. I was wondering what she was trying to get at, and
finally she comes up at about one o'clock and she tells me,
"When are the painters going to come?" She says, "the painters." "Well, you called," I said, "and James told you I was the
one that was going to paint your house." Then she says, "Well,
no, if I had wanted a woman painter, I could have hired my
niece." So it really got me, you know. I felt terrible, and I told
her, "Well, if you still want her, you can go get her. I'll gladly
disappear from here." So she says, "No, you might as well finish
the job." But I felt real bad.

All in all, though, right now everything's fine. I've only got
five kids left at home, and it's kind of a relief because they get out
and work some, too. My oldest daughter wants to go out to work
with me, do what I do, so I told her I was going to let her try this
summer. She's sixteen. She's already worked in a restaurant for
three years, from when she gets out of school, to nine or ten. This
year I told her I wanted her to quit, so she can catch up on her
schoolwork. I don't know if any of them will go to college. I'm
not going to force them to go, but it would be nice if they would.

Anyway, I'm feeling really good right now. I don't have as
many responsibilities, I don't have to work all the time. Every
once in a while I take a day off and go treasure hunting up in the
mountains. So far, I've only found a few broken bottles. This
lady up in Madrid wanted them, so I'm going to start saving them
for her. For myself, the only thing I really care to find is old coins.
I have a hobby of old coins, and I take a metal detector with me.
This summer I want to go treasure hunting to a certain place I
heard about. You need a jeep to get up there, so I'm going to rent

one, and I'm going to stay over there for about two weeks—and I'll rest at the same time, because sometimes I really like being by myself.

I guess I'm a person of many moods. I just like to do different things. So far, my best job has been painting, but I want to go back to school and take typing or office work for when I get older. Because I know I ain't always going to have the strength for this.

This fall I'm going to get married. I'll keep working for a little while after that, but then I have this dream. I want to buy forty acres of land up in Edgewood, and I want my kids to help me build a home all by ourselves, similar to the antique home we used to live in, up in the mountains. I want to make all the *adobe*s, then I want to build a double-wall *adobe* home, and part of the furniture is going to be *adobe*, too. My husband can help, but only if he doesn't get in the way of my ideas. He does like to get into my ideas, but this is my dream, the only dream I have—those forty acres in Edgewood, and build my dream house there.

# Jennie Montoya

Jennie Montoya read to us from a poem she had written about her grandmother: "*Rabanitos, sus cachetes,/ su risa robusta, sensual/ del mundo* . . . (Her cheeks as radishes,/ her laughter robust, sensuous/ worldly . . .)." A student, a writer, a mother, and a wife, Jennie Montoya lives with her husband and two children in a house in the northern valley of Albuquerque, not far from the countryside where she was born. Now in her thirties, she attempts to balance the demands of graduate school and her responsibilities to her family and community, while striving to define her life and the life of "my people, *la Raza.*"

MY EARLIEST YEARS WERE SPENT in Los Griegos, the small farming community where I was born, just north of Albuquerque. For a long time I was the only child there, and because my mother worked as a maid, I was raised as a communal child. My grandma, all my *primos* and my *tíos* and my *tías*, (cousins, uncles and aunts) took care of me. Life there was very communal. Everybody had two or four acres that they'd farm, and they shared all their goods. If one had an oversupply of apples, they would trade it with another, who would give cherries, or whatever they had. It went on like that all summer. In the fall people helped each other out with *matanzas.* They got up early in the morning to slaughter. Then they helped throughout the day preparing the meat for winter. The land was open, and everybody worked in each other's area. The only fences we had were for the pigs and the goats. Chickens ran all over the place. We might coop them up during the ripening season, but after that, what fell from the trees was the chickens'. It was very beautiful there in those days; there was no competitiveness.

In my family, school was always emphasized as the way to economic equality. Being a domestic, my mother never made very much money, but whatever she made was for me, and she never let me work. She said my job was to make good grades in school. Then, in the summer, I was to stay around the house and help with the chores and the farm work. So I got good grades and stayed home. I'd help my grandma in the fields, or pumping the water, chopping the wood, whatever.

Then in the sixties the developers came in, and the whole community was disrupted. That's the first time I wrote a poem. I was seventeen and it was an angry poem about the Dale Bellamah development. We had this beautiful field of alfalfa right next to our *barrio*, with huge cottonwood trees all along the irrigation ditch. Of course, the field didn't belong to us. It belonged to the *Anglo patrón*, but I always felt it was our field. One day the development people came in, when I was in high school, and cut down all those trees. I remember crying about it, because they were cutting the limbs, and it was like they were cutting my limbs off. My mother found me crying and she said, "What's wrong? Why are you crying?" And I said, "Mom, they're cutting the trees down. Why are they cutting these beautiful trees down? I don't understand it." Of course, it was because they were starting this upper-class housing area for *Anglos* and out-of-state people. That was the start of my poetry. Basically, it started because I couldn't stand the idea of outsiders coming in and disrupting our area.

I finished high school at eighteen, and my mother said, "Well, what are you going to do now? This is as far as I can help you. You're on your own. If you want to go to business college, that's fine." Well, I was typing twenty-five words per minute when I graduated, and I couldn't stand it. "No, Mom," I said, "I really want to go to college." And she said, "Huh? That's really expensive. That's out of our world." And it was, but I really wanted to go because I wanted to be an English teacher and come back and teach Shakespeare to my Chicanos. I was in love with Shakespeare. I didn't know there was Don Quixote. Nobody told me that Chicanos had written classics. Nobody told me that Gabriela Mistral had won a Nobel Prize.* So I assumed that the only language in the world for creating classics was English.

At UNM I took my first Spanish class. I had always been bilingual, but it had never occurred to me to write in Spanish. That first semester I went insane! I started writing in Spanish immediately. My first Spanish poem was a feminist poem talking about how women shouldn't just pretend to become liberated

---

* Gabriela Mistral, a Chilean poet, won the Nobel prize for literature in 1945, the first Latin American to receive this distinction.

by liberating themselves from things like housework, but we should go on to create new ideas, "Don't reach for the moon but go out and reach for the stars." Since that first semester I have been writing in Spanish, and it's really difficult for me to go back and express myself in English.

I've always been politically aware, but I didn't become politically active until my senior year in college. That's when I met my husband, at a grape boycott meeting.* He was a VISTA worker at the time.† We were married right after my graduation. I couldn't get a job in the Albuquerque public schools, so the first two years of our marriage I worked as a bookkeeper for a Chicano contractor. This was the first time I had an opportunity to go into the real world and see how this society runs. It runs on money—what an insight! Those first two years were really good, though, because I was writing all the time, after work or when I was alone on weekends. I had a lot of free time then, and I really miss that now.

When my first child came, I was teaching Chicano literature at the university and studying for my master's. I was teaching on Tuesdays and Thursdays. I would leave my child with my mother or my mother-in-law and try to cram everything into those two days. Finally, when I had my second child two years later, I decided to stay home, and I've been home for the past year.

I consider my work now to be raising my children to be whole human beings. That's what has to take priority now. But I look at it this way: the first two years of my married life my priority was to be a lover—I think I succeeded at that. Now, I think my role is to be a mother for the next five or six years. If I can do concentrated work with my children, teaching them the basics of how to get along and have good morals before the school system takes over, I think that's all one woman can do.

* The grape boycott, a nationwide consumer boycott of grapes, was organized by the United Farmworkers in 1967 to pressure major grape growers to bargain with the Farmworkers Union. The boycott led growers to sign their first contracts with the union in 1970.

† Volunteers In Service To America, or VISTA, is a community service organization, funded by the federal government, which pays volunteer workers a subsistence wage to work in grass-roots community development groups.

I have been home for this past year, but I have been going to school part-time, too. I'm only about thirteen hours away from my master's. I go to school in the late afternoon and either my husband or one of the grandmas takes care of the kids. But I have to be very careful to assert myself because my husband does expect me to come home and take care of the children, and when I'm home they do depend on me. This takes away from my study time. I have to assert myself about that and say, "I'm going to the library this evening to study. I will come back at eight or nine."

I'm still writing my poetry, too. I would prefer to do just that if I could afford it. If money would drop from heaven, I would go on being a writer. But I have to depend on teaching and on getting my degree. So in my working hours I'm usually doing research or reading books for my courses. I do my own writing when I'm half asleep, my husband's attacking me, my children are crying—and I'm sitting there trying to grab for paper to remember ideas. Or I try to write things late at night, or during *Sesame Street,* or when I'm drinking my last cup of coffee in the morning.

I write two kinds of poetry, *Anglo* poetry, which is sometimes very angry, and then simply poetry about my people. The poetry about my people is all positive. I try to put all the negative aspects of our culture to the background. Not that our culture is perfect, but it's important to take the positive aspects and nourish them, keep them alive. That's one of the reasons that I write in Spanish—because I realize that we have to retain the Spanish language instead of becoming Anglicized. I'm also working on a novel. I've been working on it for the past four years. It's going to be a *Gone With the Wind* type, about the parts I can remember from our culture and about the old people.

After my children are in school and I've finished my novel, I would either like to go to law school or finish my Ph.D. Whatever is going to be more important to our people. Right now literature is important to me because I think the pen is my only sword, but we're going to need more lawyers, because our people are losing their land so fast, and for many other reasons. So I think that would be a good vocation, too.

So this is my work at the moment—my children, my husband, my courses, and my writing. How do I find time for everything?

I fight with my husband. I ignore my children. And I have all the guilt that comes down upon a woman trying to liberate herself.

Seriously, I can't separate my work from my life. If my mother needs me, I have to put the pen down. I've got to go see what my mother wants. My God! I can't say, "Mother, I'm sorry. I'm working on my novel." Or if my uncle says, "We're working here in the yard and we need your truck," "Okay," and here I go with the truck. My people are the priority. Our work is an integral part of us. I can't see saying, "I'm going to become a poet and write beautiful things," because that's not the reality. The reality is my people, the reality is what I am. I am a Chicana, with all the social, political, and economic implications that come with it.

# FOUR:
# A
# LIGHTED
# FIRE

*Las lumbres
que prendo
no las
apagarán.*

The fires
I light
will never
be put out.

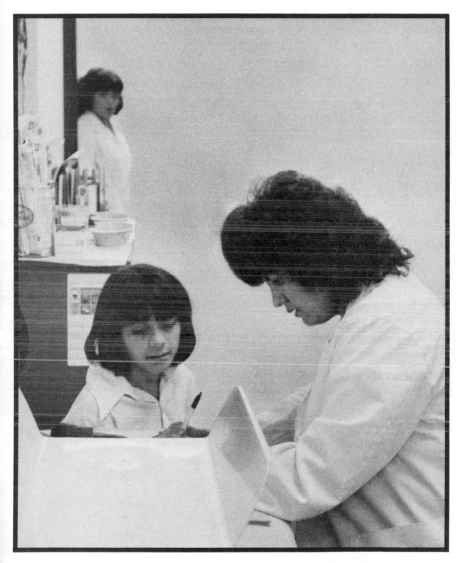

The view at top left is the setting for *La Cooperativa Agrícola del Pueblo de Tierra Amarilla*, a self-help venture growing out of militant Chicano struggle. Valentina Valdez, bottom left, directs *La Cooperativa*, which includes a medical and dental clinic, a legal aid program, and other services. At right: many miles south, a Hispanic health worker and patient in an Albuquerque clinic.

Many young Hispanas graduate into clerical or assembly line jobs at factories such as the one pictured at left; others, like the University of New Mexico student at right, are seeking new opportunities through higher education, often working meanwhile at part-time jobs. Whether in classroom, factory, or other work, these women frequently link hopes for their own advancement with concern for the advancement of other Hispanas and *la Raza*.

Lulu Turrietta, left, is happy with her choice of
working at home as mother and wife; but she decidedly
approves of freedom and equality for women, and can
imagine that her two daughters may choose lives
quite different from hers. She is planning her family
in order to enjoy her children, and to concentrate on
developing their abilities. Singer Debbie Martínez,
right, just out of her teens and a professional since
the age of twelve, has done increasingly well in the
competitive world of entertainment. She is interested
in using her music to help preserve Hispanic folk
culture and to build Chicano pride. Both young women
feel a deep attachment to their ethnic roots.

THE YOUNGEST WOMEN WE INTERVIEWED talked of the differences between their lives and the lives of their mothers and grandmothers. They spoke of the ways in which their culture has changed over the generations, but they also told us of traditions that have not died, of rural customs still practiced by the people in the city *barrios.*

Born during the fifties and early sixties, most of these young women grew up in Albuquerque. In an environment dominated by *Anglo* culture, the majority of them were taught to use English as their first language. Those whose first language was Spanish described being discriminated against in school—as had the older generations of women—by teachers and principals who saw them as problem students. Not until the late sixties were bilingual educational programs instituted in some New Mexico elementary schools; but that development came too late for this generation of women, several of whom expressed the hope that their own children would be able to "keep their language."

Many of the young women we interviewed had finished high school and are now supporting themselves as bank tellers, secretaries, teachers' aides, or assembly-line workers; others are working their way through college. Some, in their late twenties, have completed their professional training as teachers or librarians. Often these Hispanas reported that even with diplomas and higher degrees they had met institutional and personal discrimination when looking for employment. "It took me a long time to understand that there was still racism in this country," said Valentina Valdez, now twenty-nine, "and that even though I had graduated from high school, the only kind of job that people were going to hire a Chicana for was waitressing or cleaning jobs you don't really even need a high school diploma for."

Valentina Valdez's remark was seconded by a librarian who is working as a secretary. "In terms of my education I'm not especially typical of my race. I've had alternatives other Chicanas haven't had. But then, I think I am typical in that even after I've finished my degree—look at the kind of job I have."

Several of the younger women we interviewed are mothers. Some work at home, taking care of their families, and some have returned to paying jobs. Others are single mothers totally responsible for the emotional and financial support of their children. "When I got my job at Lenkhurt, it was a real switch," reported Maria Ávila, a single mother and a factory worker. "Suddenly I was doing everything, raising a child, working and taking care of the house . . . it felt real good because I didn't have to ask anybody for anything."

Many women are planning lives that they hope will include both children and a career. "Eventually," said Debbie Martinez, a professional singer, "I would like to reach the point where I can call my own shots, work at my own pace and still be secure in my career. Also, maybe I'm being idealistic, but I'd like to have a family, too."

Young Hispanas today are able to choose more varied ways of living and of making a living than were open to their mothers and grandmothers. Yet through this new variety of experience runs a strong thread of identification with Hispanic life and tradition. Debbie Martinez's singing career is built around Spanish songs about the people and the land of New Mexico. Lulu Turrietta talks of feeling close to her mother's life as she stays at home to rear her children, while Irene García, a dentistry student, describes the unfailing understanding and support of her grandmother. At seventeen, Cathy Baca is increasingly interested in the Chicano movement, and also hopes some day to visit Cuba; meanwhile, she works with troubled teenagers, most of them Hispanic, and, "Every day I teach one person something new."

*Ayúdale a la gente.* "Help the people." The young women in this section look back to their origins and also to the future, as did their mothers and grandmothers before them, hoping to make a better path for generations of Hispanas who will follow.

# Valentina Valdez

Twenty-nine-year-old Valentina Valdez lives "up north" in Tierra Amarilla, a Hispanic village first established in 1832 by Mexican and Spanish farmers. Born in Colorado, Valentina Valdez moved to New Mexico to join the *Alianza Federal de las Mercedes*, a group working to return land-grants to the families of their original owners. She subsequently joined with several other *Alianza* workers to organize a small farming cooperative. Today, *La Cooperativa de Tierra Amarilla* has grown to include a community-run medical clinic, a dental clinic, and a legal office. As the organization has expanded, so have Valentina Valdez's responsibilities, and she is now the director of the cooperative.

I WAS BORN in the town of San Luis in 1948, the oldest of six kids. My father had a barbershop. He did okay with it for a while. But then when I was about eleven years old, he became involved in the land-grant struggle, and little by little he started losing customers.* Our family became very poor and all of us kids were expected to help out. We had a lot of chores. Hauling wood and water, planting, working in the fields.

My father was always talking about the Spanish land grants—how the land had been stolen from Chicanos by the *Anglos* and the government. I didn't believe him. I was real patriotic and I didn't believe that could happen in the United States. So a lot of the time I thought, "He's crazy," or, "He's going crazy."

Finally a lot of customers just wouldn't go to the barbershop and he gave up trying to make it. We had to sell the house and the land for back taxes because my parents couldn't meet the payments any more. It was a real loss, losing the land and the house they had worked on so hard.

My father started looking for work in other places, other towns. In a lot of rural Chicano families the father would go off

---

* For a brief indication of the background of the Spanish land grant struggle, see the footnote on page 54.

for work while the mother stayed at home with the kids, took care of the farm—but neither he nor my mother liked the concept of the family being separated. So, finally, we all moved to Denver.

I was fourteen when we moved. That was a real culture shock for me. At first I was real happy to be moving away from all those chores. But the people in Denver were so different. My brothers, my sisters, and I went to Abraham Lincoln High School. It was predominantly white. Maybe an eighth of the students were Chicano. Many of the teachers there were racist. It was really bad. My grades were so down in the dumps. I really hated school but I had made up my mind that I was going to graduate because I thought I had to, to get a good job.

I must have been about sixteen or seventeen when this TV program came out on Spanish-Americans. Here was this professor on TV saying that Spanish-Americans were poor because they were lazy, superstitious, ignorant—the whole bit. They showed cardboard houses that were falling apart with beautiful cars out front. My dad was just furious. That TV show made a really big impression on me, and I think that's what made me snap.

The morning after that show we were studying the Treaty of Guadalupe Hidalgo in history class and there was just this paragraph in the book that said that the treaty gave New Mexico to the United States. The teacher asked if we'd seen the program. A few kids raised their hands and the teacher said, "Well, how did you like it?" Everybody said, "I liked it." That made me feel really bad. I wanted to say something but I didn't have anything together, so I couldn't answer them.

After class, though, I started organizing a group of women. I said, "Why don't we make a report about exactly what happened, and what we think, and we can get extra credit?" Everybody wanted to do that, so I told my dad I was going to make a report on the Treaty of Guadalupe Hidalgo. And oh! He was so happy that he helped me. It took me about two months to get all the articles and things together.

It was the end of the semester when I finished. By then the others had all drifted away and left me by myself. It was the first time that I had ever done anything like this, and I was afraid that the teacher would be furious and the kids would just pound me with questions. I was sweating. I was trembling, but I gave the report. I did it!

I told them that the TV show was wrong. It wasn't true that our people were lazy and superstitious. We were poor because our land had been stolen and we always got the worst-paying jobs, producing food, working in the mines, and building roads. I told them how the King of Spain had issued land grants to the Spanish and Mexican people who first came to this territory. Then I told them how the treaty was signed in 1848 when New Mexico became a territory of the United States and how it was supposed to guarantee the Spanish and Mexican heirs all their rights to the land-grant lands. But then, when New Mexico became a state and the laws were changed to English, a lot of people couldn't understand the English laws and Chicanos lost over four million acres of land-grant territory. I ended up talking about today and the fact that people now have to buy permits from the National Forest Service to graze their cattle on the land that once belonged to their ancestors.

Well, when I got done with that report the teacher was just overwhelmed. He was really happy. He went around telling all the other teachers what a good job I'd done. "You just have to hear this girl. She gave this fantastic report." He was so excited. I felt really good.

When I graduated from high school, I couldn't get a good job even though I had a diploma. That had a big impact on me. It really helped me to see that things weren't the way they'd been painted through school. I got so upset that I decided to volunteer and come over here to work with the *Alianza Federal de las Mercedes*, a group of Chicanos that had gotten together to fight for their rights to the original land grants and to try and protect Chicano farmers from losing even more land and from losing their grazing rights in the National Forests.

When I told my father, he was really thrilled. He was so happy that at last he'd broken through to one of his kids—he backed me all the way. But he was real strict. He came over here with me and made sure that I stayed with an elderly family, the whole bit.

I arrived about two months before the courthouse raid when
*Alianza* members attempted to place the district attorney of Rio
Arriba county under citizens' arrest for improperly imprisoning
several land-grant activists. The state government brought in
the National Guard and tanks and helicopters. They penned up
hundreds of people. I wasn't on the scene; I was taking care of
the office. It was the only place that people knew, to get hold
of the raiders and other *Alianza* members and get information.
We had direct communication with the media and with the
people that were coming in from all over the country to participate and support the raid.

That summer was important. It brought up the issue of land
grants to the nation and to the world. I think that was really positive. Chicanos started getting more jobs and a lot of federal programs started coming in. To me, there's stages—people have
to go through rallies, riots, demonstrations, that type of thing.
Then, after that, it goes to organizing, starting alternatives for
poor people to see that we can create, control, and manage for
ourselves instead of having it come down from the government.
We can implement good programs that serve us.

During that first summer I had gotten really close to one of the
men in the *Alianza*, and after a while we started living together.
He was much older than I was, and I guess in a way he took
care of me, taught me things.

A couple of years later, my husband and I and some of the other
people who'd been active in the land-grant struggle started organizing *La Cooperativa Agrícola del Pueblo de Tierra Amarilla*.
The land-grant heirs lent us some of their land and we set up a
camp on five hundred acres that one man had reclaimed from
some whites in Texas. In the beginning we all lived in tents and
we cooked outside. There was about six to twelve people who
volunteered full-time. Then the community people used to help
us whenever they could—when they didn't have to work to get
salaries, to pay for their houses, and to pay their bills.

Some of the land hadn't been worked in thirty-five years. The
ground was so hard that a tractor would stand on end. In other
places, we had to clear off the *chamiso* (sagebrush) and the
trees. But that first year we planted about fifty acres of land.

We planted potatoes, wheat, onions, corn, and peas. All summer we'd go out and weed, come back to camp, eat supper, and sing by the fire. It was hard work but it was good. We harvested three hundred hundred-pound sacks of potatoes, plus all the other vegetables.

In July of that first year we heard that the doctor in Tierra Amarilla was putting his clinic up for sale, for forty-one thousand dollars. We had just started the *cooperativa* and we didn't know where we would get the money, but we went to see if he would sell it to us. From our experience in the Alianza we knew there were people interested in helping people to help themselves, so we went around the state asking for funds and that summer we bought the clinic.

We had a really hard time getting it started. Less than ten days after we bought it, some arsonists burned it down. So we had to rebuild it. That took about six months. Then we didn't want to charge people any more than they could afford to pay. If they couldn't pay money, we wanted them to be able to pay with stock or produce or by doing volunteer work at the clinic. So it took us a long time to find a doctor and nurses because we were looking for people who could work seven days a week, twenty-four hours a day, for just room and board. We finally got this one doctor who donated a year of his services. Then we got another doctor to replace him. After a couple of years we began paying salaries, real low salaries, but we were beginning to pay. All along we've had this policy that everyone makes the same salary whether they're receptionists, doctors, janitors, or nurses. So with our first salaries, all the couples got a hundred and fifty a month and the single people got seventy-five. Little by little it went up. Now we're at five hundred dollars a month.

We've really expanded our program too. We've got two doctors and one physician's assistant, a dentist and a person who does the lab work in dentistry, an X ray lab technician, two receptionists, a bookkeeper and a manager—that's me.

We've always had the policy of training people from the community. Under the supervision of the doctors and the licensed nurses, they've learned how to do lab work, give shots, deliver babies, keep books, things like that. Now we've also started an *oficina de ley* (law program). It's similar to a legal aid program, except that we handle a wider variety of cases.

I've had to learn all the rules and regulations of the welfare program, learn about food stamps, supplemental income, Social Security, and veterans benefits, so that I could be an advocate for people on those programs. Learning to be a good manager has been really hard for me. I've also had the problem of being the manager of a worker-run organization. I have to tell people that I used to work with on an equal basis, "Well, you're going to do this now and if you don't do it, you're going to get laid off or fired."

There have been personal problems too. My husband was twenty-eight years older than me. I was so young when I met him. I was just a baby, and I didn't have a lot of ideas of my own. Up to a certain point he really encouraged me to be active, but he never really wanted me to go out and do things for myself. For the first six years we lived together, he told me when I could go places. I would have to ask permission. Then I just got tired of it and said, "Look, I'm going to do it whether you like it or not." We started having more problems and a year and a half ago, after living together for ten years, we separated.

To me that kind of sexism is really awful. I wish that's something they'd teach you about in schools, because sexism is just like racism. It's a part of the system. It's a part of the way that everything's set up in this country. It doesn't just happen to me.

As a matter of fact, I know very few couples who can both be active and still communicate with each other. There's not a lot of negotiating, and it seems like divorce is the only answer for women who really get active in something. It's so bad to break up the family and cause so many other problems with the kids. But I think it's really important for women to make it clear that they're separate individuals with different interests. At the co-op we have regular women's meetings to talk about the problems of raising children, splitting up, whatever. During the ten years I've been involved in the movement I've met some really independent women and they've had a major effect on my life. They've helped me a lot in my development as a woman and as a worker. If they hadn't been there, I would probably still be with my husband and he would probably still be telling me what to do, and worse.

So it seems it's always an uphill struggle. Sometimes I stop to think about what my life would have been if I hadn't taken this route. I don't know. I think it would have been pretty boring.

# Irene García

Reared in a family of twelve children, Irene García has been supporting herself financially since she was fifteen. Today, at twenty-four,
she is a predental student at the University of Albuquerque. Irene
García is a lesbian. Here she speaks of her plans both for a career and
for a way of life that were not options for women of her mother's
generation.

I WAS RAISED UP IN A VERY STRICT FAMILY. My father was excep-
tionally strict with us kids and my mother followed along with
him. There were twelve kids in our family—my five brothers
and sisters and me, then the six kids that were born after me.
When I was little, I thought they were my brothers and sisters,
too, but they weren't.

See, I was always told that my father was García—he's the
father of the last six kids in our family—but my older brothers
and sisters always seemed to be really different from my younger
ones. Well, when I got to be thirteen I was very curious about all
this. I asked my mom about it, but she closed up immediately—
wouldn't tell me anything. So I went to my grandmother and
asked her. She told me that my real father's name was Baca and
that the first six of us were his kids. I can't remember Baca well,
but my grandma says he used to beat my mother. He was an alcoholic and he used to waste all our money on gambling and drinking. Finally my mother left him and married García. That's the
man I was taught to call my father.

When I was very, very little I used to live with my grandmother, my mother's mother. She lived in a very old house by
the irrigation ditch. She was very poor. I remember sleeping on
the floor on cushions and waking up to cockroaches. We used to
go to this big building down by the railroad tracks to get our
commodity foods. They'd give us powdered milk and cans of peanut butter—stuff like that. We'd put all the food in this little cart
and pull it back home. My grandmother spoiled me to death,
though. She really liked me. I became real close to her, and she
used to tell me all sorts of private things that I wasn't supposed
to be told. This got my mom upset, but my grandma didn't care.

After a year or two I moved back in with my mother. She had a couple more kids by then. It seemed year after year she just kept having them. She was a very strong Catholic and she didn't believe in birth control, not until after she started thinking she couldn't afford all of us. Then she and my father went to talk to the priest about it. The priest said, "No," and my mom said, "Well, I'm sorry, but you'll have to accept me for what I am, for what I want to do, rather than listening to what God says all the time." That was it, but by then she'd had twelve children. At that time my father was a cashier at Kelly's supermarket and he just couldn't make any money. Then he took a government test of some kind and he became a mail carrier. We started coming up in the world. We got better clothes and more things to play with. I just couldn't understand it—to go from picking up commodity foods to buying things at the store. It was this huge change and I felt, man! we're really high-class now. Actually, we were still lower middle class, but I didn't know that.

School was really hard for me in the beginning. When I went to first grade I didn't speak any English, and even after three years I still didn't know it well, so they put me in special ed. I hated that. I only stayed there a couple of years, but even now I don't feel comfortable in English and I don't think I ever will. It's hard for me to pronounce a lot of the words. I still remember sitting in class and wanting to raise my hand, but I couldn't because maybe I'd say something wrong.

When I went to junior high I became best friends with this *Anglo* girl, Dorothy. We really liked each other and we used to do everything together. That is, until we got to high school. In my high school you just didn't hang around with *Anglo* kids if you were a Chicana. You stayed with your own nationality, because if you didn't, you'd get beaten up. So, after junior high, we stopped hanging around together.

I started going out with guys when I was about twelve or thirteen, but I was never really crazy about them. I never noticed guys on the street or on TV. It was always the women I was attracted to. I never really thought about being gay either. As a matter of fact, I even made fun of gay people because all my friends did. At least I made fun of them until I became gay, which was when I was about fourteen.

That's when I had my first lesbian experience. It was with a student about a year older than I was. We were taking showers after basketball practice and she came in and kissed me. She surprised me, and I got very scared. Here I was standing stark naked taking a shower, and she jumped in and kissed me! I just didn't know how to handle it, but then we talked for a while and things turned out okay. Sexually, I liked it, but at the same time I felt funny. I felt queer. I felt people were going to reject me. I felt like a queer. Queer. I felt strange. Later, when I met other lesbian women and found out what lesbians were all about, it was okay. I felt more comfortable about it. I still dated guys some when I was in high school, but mostly I went out with women. *unusually sense of clarity*

The summer when I was about fifteen I got a job at Lovelace-Bataan Hospital as a nursing assistant. I was making good money, and I got an apartment with another woman who was working there, and I loved it. I felt like I was really settled, fifteen going on sixteen. I bought a car and I decided that I wanted to go to college so that I could be a nurse.

At about that time I opened up to my mother and told her I'd had relationships with women. At first she couldn't understand—none of my family could. They kept bugging me—why couldn't I be like the Candelaria girls down the street? It was this huge family of girls who always dressed up in all these girly clothes and stuff—nice, but just not my style. I've always been a tomboy, jeans and T-shirts and old raggedy tennis shoes.

Anyway, after I talked to my mother for a while, she finally accepted that I was gay and she opened up to me. She admitted that she had been a homosexual woman when she was younger. My grandma showed me a picture of her. She used to ride motorcycles and wear men's pants. She was a real tough woman and she was really beautiful, gorgeous. But women back then couldn't make it alone. That was the whole thing. Either you got married or you died. They didn't have any benefits for women, and you couldn't get into school unless your father had money. And on top of that, my mom didn't have that much education. She only went up to the fourth or fifth grade. *G's economic dependence on men— as well as cultural prejudices—discourage a ♀ from coming out & living her life*

Little by little, most of the rest of my family accepted it, too, my brothers and my little sisters. Even today, my grandma thinks I'm the only intelligent woman in the family because I

*so Race, Class, Compound this oppression*

don't want to get married and go out and have kids. My mother respects me for the same reason. She tells my little sisters, "Don't get married right off. Go on—go to school and do something with yourself. Then get married if you want to."

Well, as I said, I'd already decided that I wanted to go to college. And, when I was eighteen, I started going to UNM. I did really well my first year. Then I transferred over to the University of Albuquerque because I was interested in nursing and I thought they had a better program.

The first year I was there, though, I fell in love, and I mean really in love. I'd never felt like that about anyone before. We went together for six months and when we broke up it was awful for me. I was still in love with her, and I used to go out and drink all the time. I quit my job, I dropped out of school. It was awful.

Then I worked for a while, got me a new car and saved my money for school again. I just got my head together. I felt that I had to do it—nobody else was going to do it for me. I went back to school. I decided to get out of nursing, and I switched into the predental program. Then, Diana, the woman I was in love with, and I went back together. We moved into an apartment together and things are better now.

Right now, with Diana and me, it's almost like we're married. We went out and got rings together and our money's our money, no matter who earns it. We both pay the bills. And it's a lot like a heterosexual marriage except that in some ways I think we're freer than people in a real marriage. To me, a woman-and-a-woman relationship is really, really different from a man and a woman. It's hard to explain it, but it's very easy to feel it. When you start a relationship with a man, you know what you're supposed to do with the house and everything. You know your routines because you were brought up that way. With a lesbian relationship, you have to build a whole new system and figure out your own way of doing things. But it's good, too, because you don't feel so trapped. If you don't like it, you can leave.

I think it's probably harder to get out of a marriage. Personally, I think marriage should be abandoned—I guess mainly because I am afraid of being trapped. I would like to see a woman-to-woman commitment, not marriage. Really, I guess that's what I have with Diana right now, a commitment. We know we want to be together now. And when we graduate, we're planning to move out to San Francisco together. She wants to go to med school out there, and I want to go to dental school. But beyond that, who knows?

When I think of the future on a large scale—not just Diana and me—I would like to see more of a woman's world. I think we need more businesswomen, congresswomen, women that can talk, so that we can get our rights. In my largest fantasies, I would love to see a woman president.

*wants social change, but doesn't seem aware of oppression among ♀, by ♂*

→ *doesn't look @ the fact that, just like marriage, lesbians act out gender assoc'd roles - butch/femme. We can be oppressive. Internalized gender oppression, disrespect & hatred for ♀.*

(see Maya p.42)

# Lulu Turrietta

"You should talk to my nephew's wife, Lulu," Josephine Turrietta
had told us. "She works in the house with her family. She still works
the way I worked, and the way my mother worked too." Lulu Turrietta is
twenty-four. She lives with her husband, Joe, an auto mechanic.
They have two young daughters, whose development Lulu Turrietta
sees as a responsibility, a challenge, and a delight.

I'VE ALWAYS FELT REALLY CLOSE to my mother and really close to
my aunt and to my grandmother—all the women in my family.
I'm the oldest of six kids—three boys and three girls—and when
I was very little, me and my cousin used to go over to my grandmother's to play. She'd make us dolls out of rags and then she'd
make us little brooms and a little stove, and we'd go out into the
garage and we'd stay there all day playing *comadres*. Then, every
year on the day before Christmas, me and my mother and my
cousins and my grandma would all go over to my aunt's house
and we'd make *chile rellenos, empanadas,* and *posole* to get
ready for the *nacimiento* (Nativity). So, we were all really close,
and we had a really good time together.

Things weren't quite so happy in our own house, though—
my mom's house. My dad used to be really mean to my mom. He
played the saxophone in a band, and I used to hear him come
home at four in the morning and accuse her of going out. And I
knew it wasn't true. But my mom took this ever since I was
small. Then, one night when I was nine years old, he came home
and he really beat her up. She was black and blue. So I went to her
and I said, "Ma, all the kids are crying and I don't like this. Why
don't you leave him?" My mom says when I told her this I was
talking to her just like a big person, and I said, "Ma, please, leave
him a note and just go." Well, a little bit after that, she did.

She left him and she started bringing us up all by herself—all
six of us. My youngest sister was only nine months old. For a long
time after that, we lived on welfare. Sometimes she'd find work,
but most of the time we were on welfare and it was really hard on
her. My younger brother and I used to help her all we could. We'd
clean for her and we'd take care of the little ones when she went
shopping.

When I was about fourteen I got a job working at Casa Angelica after school so that I could help out with the bills. I'd come home from school at two-thirty and go to work at three. Then I'd get off at seven, come home and try to do my homework, but I was always real tired, and I got 'way behind in my work. Finally, I asked my mother if I could quit school and go to work full-time. She said, "Well, I don't know, *mi'jita*," because she'd always thought that our education was really important. When we were little, she always used to be a room mother and everything. But I told her, "Ma, I never liked school anyway." And that was true. I never did. So when I got to be sixteen, I quit school and got a job working full-time in a day-care center.

After my mom got the divorce she didn't go out with guys for about four or five years. She'd just stay with us kids all the time. Finally, when I was about twelve or thirteen, she started dating, going out to dances, things like that. Sometimes I'd stay with the kids for her or she'd stay with the kids while I went out.

We were very close to each other, and she was always very open with me about guys and about sex. I remember I used to come home from a date, or from going out with the girls. I'd go into her bedroom to see if she were awake, and she'd sit up in bed and say, "How was your date? Did you have fun?" and we'd talk.

When I was about seventeen I met Joe and really liked him. I remember telling my mom, "Oh, I get the chills when I see him, ma" and she told me, "Good, *mi'jita*, just act natural with him; don't worry." Well, she was asleep when I got home on the night Joe brought me the engagement ring. When I woke her up to show her the ring, she was so happy for me that she started crying. Then I started crying and we must have stayed up the whole night, talking and crying.

A few months later Joe and I got married and he told me my work was at home and to quit my job. So I did, and I've been home ever since. In the beginning, it was really boring because I didn't have anything to do. But then Joanna was born and that made things different. Everything was more exciting. Joe and I had something to share. Joanna brought us closer together. She was just so much fun to do things with.

She's a big girl now—she's five. But when she was little, I used to get her paper and crayolas and paint, and I taught her how to color and to write her name and draw a face. She loved to study, and she still does. Over at the kindergarten, the teachers say they're really surprised with her because she does so well. She's second in her class, and I'm really proud of her. I'm going to start working with the baby, Susie, soon, because I think it's really important.

I really wish I could teach the girls to speak Spanish. I spoke it when I was growing up. I tried to teach it to Joanna when she was a baby, but Joe doesn't speak it. And you know, it just doesn't work when only one person is speaking it. To talk Spanish, you need the whole family behind you.

I've always wanted four kids and I still do. But I don't want any more right away. I don't like the idea of having my kids all lumped together. There's four years between Joanna and Susie, and I like it that way, because then I get to spend time with each of them and enjoy everything they do.

I think things are different nowadays, different from when I was growing up. A lot of girls are staying in school now. They're getting equal to men, and I think it's a good thing, too, because they're going to need their education. They're the ones that have to be ultimately responsible for the kids. The men aren't.

Now with my own two, I can't tell about Susie yet because she's still a baby, but Joanna has a real mind of her own. I get the feeling that when she grows up, she's going to leave me and get an apartment or something. Nowadays it doesn't seem as if girls are getting married as much as they used to. It seems very free, and nobody talks about it much. So Joanna might not even get married. I wouldn't force her to get married, but I hope she doesn't get pregnant without getting married. It's so hard to support kids by yourself. I watched my mother do that after her divorce and it's hard.

I still see a lot of my mother, and we talk to each other on the phone every day. I feel my life is really close to hers. I've always wanted a big family, and I've always wanted to bring up my kids the way she brought us up. Only, for me, it's so much easier than it was for my mother. She was all by herself with six kids, while I've got Joe, and the house, and I can plan my babies. I always told my mom that I was going to settle down when I was eighteen, and I did. Now I'm just really happy, and I wouldn't trade my life for anything.

# Debbie Martínez

Debbie Martínez has been singing since she was twelve years old.
Under the professional name of "La Chicanita," she has toured
the Southwest for eight years, singing Mexican songs. Now twenty,
Debbie Martínez regards her talent as a God-given gift, and feels she
has a definite responsibility to set an example for "other young and
talented Chicanas to let them know that they can make it, it can be done."

EVER SINCE I CAN REMEMBER, I've had an ambition to sing. You
see, I come from a very musical family. My father had a *mariachi*
group called *Los Reyes de Albuquerque* (The Kings of Albuquerque). And then, when I was still very young, my older sisters
and my brother formed a group, a trio called *Los Chamacos* (The
Kids). They used to practice at home. I was about eight or nine at
the time, and I always wanted to go in there and practice with
them, but they kept kicking me out of the room. Their style was
very mellow, and I had a really strong voice. I'd just go in there
and drown them all out, so you can't blame them for not wanting
me around.

Finally, when I was about ten or eleven, I just started learning
things by myself. First I taught myself how to play the guitar. I
listened to the records we had around the house and learned a
few songs. At that time my father's group was still together, and
he used to let me play with them. Once in a while I'd get to sing
a song, but usually I just played. Then, when I was twelve, my
father decided to go on a tour of Colorado with this *mariachi*
group called the *Mariachi del Norte* (*Mariachi* of the North) and
I just pestered my father to let me go with them. Well, he was
headlining the show, so finally he said yes. I think he felt that I
was sort of going along for the ride. But I was serious. I really
loved music, and I was determined to get into it somehow or
other. At that time I didn't even have my own outfit. My sisters
had these *charro* outfits that they wore when they sang, so I bor-
rowed the skirt from one of them and the jacket from the other
and took them with me, just in case.

The night before the group's first performance in Pueblo,
everybody came over to our hotel room to practice and my father
said, "Oh, since we're just practicing, let Debbie sing a song.
We're just friends here." So I sang a song, and then the leader of

the *mariachi* said, "Well, let's put her on the show tomorrow night." It was great. We were singing for a nightclub in Pueblo, and it was just packed with people. It was really an exciting experience. And I've been singing *mariachi* music ever since. I sing *rancheros, boleros, huapangos,* and *sones*—all types of Mexican songs.

That type of music has always been very important to me. When you're very young, sometimes you view a career as fun and glamour. But in my family we were raised to be very culturally aware. At home we were all taught to speak Spanish, and I've always felt very proud to say that I was a Chicana. Many Hispanics who go into the entertainment business change their names to something not so Hispanic-sounding, like Freddie Fender, Vicki Carr, Al Hurricane. And when I was starting out people suggested that I should change my name to Debbie Martin—something like that. Well, my first name is Debbie— it has an American sound. But my last name is Martínez. And together they bring in both sides of my culture. I am an American and I'm proud of it, but I'm also of Mexican descent, which I'm also very proud of. So finally I settled on the name *La Chicanita* (Little Chicana), even though in those days the word *chicano* wasn't really accepted. *Chicanismo* (Chicano pride) was not considered a good thing; but I was proud of my heritage and I wanted to show it in my music. I believe you can use your music in many ways, and I felt that with my music I could bring a sense of pride to many people—especially the younger people. The older people already had it because that's their roots, but the younger generation often need to have it given to them. I felt that pride showed in my name, *La Chicanita.*

Basically, that's how I got my start, and I've been singing professionally for the past eight years—through junior high and high school, and now while I'm in college. It's been very important to me all along to finish my education. Many people don't realize it. They think "Oh, you already have your career. What do you need to go to college for?" Well, what if one day I can't sing? What if I lose my voice or my hearing?

Usually when I say I'm in college, people assume I'm a music major, but I'm a business major. I've had more training in music than I could have gotten in any university, and I'm already established in the music business. I don't feel a music degree could do much for me at this point, but a business degree can really help me. Today, there are so many entertainers with tremendous talent who have everything going for them except their business side. Either they don't know how to manage their careers or they get taken by sharp business people. Now, with my background in music and a knowledge of business, I can have a firm grasp on everything. I don't have to depend on someone else. Then, too, the entertainment business is kind of funny. It could go up and it could go down. A lot of it seems to be a matter of luck, and it's important to me to have my business degree to fall back on.

Singing is a very difficult field, really. Some people seem to think you hear a song, you like it, you sing it. That's all. Well, for me, it's not that easy. First of all, I don't have a regular band. So I have to learn songs that are not only appealing, but are either fairly standard band music or easy for a band to pick up. Then, too, I have to find songs that the public likes. Those aren't necessarily the ones that I like, but it really doesn't make any difference because I'm not singing them for myself. I'm singing them because I know that the people will like them.

When you're planning a show you have to have a lot of variety—fast songs, slow ones, all kinds. Because in your show you create a feeling or a mood. You may sing only six or seven songs, but with those six songs you can do a lot. I feel that your first song is the most important because that's the first impression that your audience gets, and I always choose a very happy, peppy song because that will grab an audience more than a slow or serious one. So I usually pick something like a fast *son* with a bit of dancing in the middle. Next, I'll do one that's more toned down, like a *ranchera*, still peppy but a little bit slower. Then I usually can go into a slow one. By then the audience has accepted me, and I can relax a bit. The last song is very important, too. Again, here I choose a real fast and peppy song because that's the audience's last impression of me. That's the image that will stick with them. But whenever I'm choosing songs, I always have to relate them to my image—how I want the audience to think of me.

As a matter of fact, everything a singer does relates to her image—everything from her songs to her costumes to her movements on stage presents an image. For instance, when I first started, I used to wear boots, really short skirts, and pigtails and I sang kind of childish songs. They went over really well because the public expected that. Then, when I was about sixteen or seventeen, I had to lower my skirts a bit, let my hair down, and sing songs that were a bit more serious. And now that I'm twenty, I don't wear short skirts at all. My image has changed. I'm not a little girl any more. I'm a woman and my songs reflect that. They are more sophisticated, more mature. I've also started to do some bilingual and country western songs. I'm doing more songs that are in Spanish and English, and I'm even doing some that are just English because that way I can appeal to a wider audience.

In addition to singing in nightclubs and shows, I also make records. I have four albums now. The first one was recorded when I was thirteen. My brother Lorenzo has always been my personal musical arranger. Ever since I was thirteen and he was seventeen, he's done all of the arrangements and most of the accompaniment, too. He'll play the bass, the rhythm guitars, the violins and mandolins. Usually we record in a sixteen-track studio. He plays most of the instruments, and then they dub it all in. It works out really well. You get the sound of a big band, only it's more uniform and cleaner. Recently we did one song where Lorenzo and my sister Roberta sang with me in three-part harmony. By the time we finished mixing everything, it sounded like twenty voices, but it was much clearer. It was more economical, too.

I've done performances all over New Mexico and Colorado. I've sung in Texas, the Dallas-Fort Worth area, Salt Lake City, Phoenix and Tucson, Los Angeles, and Washington, D.C. Then, just recently, I was in Mexico City, promoting my new album, *Dios, Familia y Tierra* (God, Family and Land). But it's been really difficult sometimes, working in all those performances around my schoolwork.

Next June (1980) I'll be graduating and then I'll really be free to do what I want and to dedicate a lot more time to my music. I'd sort of like to get into films and acting too—television, commercials, things like that. Eventually, what I would really like to do is reach the point where I can call my own shots, work at my own pace, and still be secure in my career. Also, maybe I'm idealistic, but I'd like to have a family, too.

You see, my own family has been so important to me, my father, my mother, my brother and my sisters. I can't stress enough how important their support has been to me. At the same time, though, it's very difficult to be married and be in the entertainment field—especially if you're a woman. You're going to be gone half the time, traveling, always in the public eye. It's very difficult to find someone understanding enough to take that. So while I do want a family of my own, I don't have any plans to get married for quite a few years.

But I think that family closeness is something really special among Chicanos. It's a closeness that I love—the warmth, the brotherhood. We're always together, and I really like that. I grew up that way, and I think it's a beautiful part of our culture.

Chicano culture is very different from *Anglo* culture. Take a Chicano wedding, for instance. We have *mariachis* there. We have special dances like *La Marcha*, special music, Chicano foods—*enchiladas, biscochitos*. It's sort of hard to identify, but there's something there that you don't often find in *Anglo* culture. There seems to be a certain distance and formality within *Anglo* families.

Something that I work for in my music is to preserve the cultural things that are unique to Chicanos. In New Mexico the culture—the customs, the music, the folklore—has been preserved. You can go into northern New Mexico and find towns that are almost untouched by time. The songs and the music—things like the *redondos*—are not Mexican or American, but original New Mexico music. They're still part of the people. They pass it on. I want to do that, too.

# Cathy Baca

Cathy Baca, seventeen, is the youngest woman speaking in *Las Mujeres*. The daughter of divorced parents, she was raised in Santa Fe by her father. She is employed now as a teacher's aide at Adelante, an alternative school for teenage drug abusers.

I DROPPED OUT OF HIGH SCHOOL when I was fifteen. I just didn't like it. I didn't like the teachers, and I didn't like the way they treated me.

I bummed around for about a year, going from program to program, and then, finally, I just got my head together and decided it was time to get my GED. So I enrolled in this alternative school called *Sueños de Esperanza* (Dreams of Hope), and I just kept studying until I passed the test. When I was going to the *Sueños* school we had this special program where all of the students would help each other study, and I got to be a really good tutor. Then one of the teachers asked me if I wanted to come over here to the sniffers' school to work as a teacher's aide—to see if I could help the sniffers, and if we could learn from each other. Well, it sounded like a good idea, so I said I'd try it.

Now, I've never been really heavy into drugs, just smoking pot and drinking, but the kids that sniff say it's a good cheap high. They take a can of spray paint and they spray it on a rag. Then they inhale it. Some of them hallucinate, and they say that when they're all sniffed up, it's like they're on a cloud. It's not addictive, though. They can stop if they want to. It's just that they have a lot of problems. They need something to do—something to remove them from their problems for a while.

Most of these kids are Chicanos. They come from the housing project for low-income people. All of their lives they've been put down because of the way they look and because they're poor. There's a lot of racism in Santa Fe, and if you're not high-class, you're nothing. They just treat you like dirt. Then, there's kids who have family problems, and problems with the cops, or kids who've gotten busted and are having trouble with their p.o.'s (parole officers).

We have about seven or eight staff people here, some part-time and some full-time. A lot of the sniffers have never gone to school day after day before, but we try to help them stay here and get their GED. Then we try to find them jobs.

Here's how the school works. The kids come in about nine o'clock and they eat breakfast. Then they start class. Class lasts until about ten-fifteen, then it's time for exercises. After exercises we come back to work, and work until eleven-forty-five, when it's time for lunch. After lunch we go down to the park for p.e., and we usually come back at about one. This is group counseling time. The kids talk to the counselors until about one-thirty and then they come back to the classroom and we give them check marks for the classes where they were good. In the afternoon there's free choice activities—arts and crafts, music, movies, extra sports, or work for money. They can do any of these until about two-thirty, and then they go home.

The kids have a lot more freedom here than they would in a regular school. That's why they like it better, and that's why they get their work done—because of the freedom. That was what I hated most about regular school—not being free to say something, not being able to talk out loud, having to raise your hand to go to the bathroom. It was a trip.

One of the reasons they asked me to work here is because I'm the same age as the students, and it's really an advantage 'cause we're sort of on the same level. I help them with their academics, and I just sort of get into everything with them. I can relate to them better than the teachers can since I'm their same age. It's far-out and they have a lot of respect for me. Usually these boys don't respect girls close to their own age, but I think they respect me because I'm working in a program like this and I'm trying to help them. They like me. Some of them have asked me out, but I won't go out with them. I wouldn't even think of it.

They learn a lot from me, though. Mostly I teach them math. I learn from them, too—they know a lot about people.

I like working in programs like this because you get a good feeling when you know you've helped somebody that really needs help. I don't know if I'll go on to be a teacher when I get older or not. I'd like to be a social worker so that I can go on helping kids like this.

These kids need a lot of people to care about them. One of their big problems is they need somebody they can trust because they've been put down so badly. You know, if I were rich and could have a school for these kids, I'd open a school up in the mountains that would be like a group home. It would be in a place that was real pretty with lots of trees—a big cabin in the wilderness, where the kids could do everything themselves. We went camping up in the wilderness a few weeks ago, and they really liked it. They could learn a lot up there—it would get them away from the city and from sniffing. They'd have their school-work to do, but there'd be other stuff to do, too, and it would be like a family.

When I get older I want to go to college, and I want to travel. I've been reading a lot about the Chicano movement and about Che Guevera. I could dig going over to Cuba to see what Che was fighting for. After that I want to get married and have kids—about five kids. I'd like to stay home and take care of them for a while, too.

But I always want to keep on working with groups like this. Right now I'm fighting for my people, and I'm working with my people, and every day I teach one person something new. Every day, and it's great!

# María Avila

At seventeen, María Avila had dropped out of high school, borne a child, and was living on welfare with her infant daughter. Two years later, she had become a full-time factory worker, a union officer, and totally responsible for herself and her daughter financially. Brought up in a traditional family, María Avila finds that her recent experiences have led her to change many of her ideas about family life, women and men, and, most of all, herself.

A LOT OF PEOPLE SAY that childhood is the best time of your life. Well, I don't agree, because when I was young I just didn't have that good a time.

School was really hard for me when I was little. In the beginning I didn't speak much English. I spoke about half and half, which might have been all right, except that most of the other kids spoke it better. So I felt dumb a lot of times. Sometimes I used to start to go to school and walk back home because I hated it so much.

Things weren't very good at home, either. My dad and my mom just didn't get along. My dad never helped my mom around the house. At dinnertime he and my brothers would sit at the table and just wait for my mom to serve them the food. I got so mad. I'd tell her not to do it. "Let them get their own," I'd say, but they were really mean to her and she was scared. There was no love between them. She just did what he told her. She was like a slave, and she depended on him because she had all these kids and she thought she couldn't leave.

All the time I was growing up I looked at men as just somebody to marry, and after seeing the way my dad treated my mom, I had some real questions about how good an idea marriage was. Then, when I was sixteen, I dropped out of school and started living with my boyfriend. He was a musician. He wanted a career in music, and he didn't want to look for a job. So, I said, "Well, if he's not going to look for a job, I'm not going to marry him." I was supporting him at the time with restaurant jobs, so I just moved out. He'd come to the house and I'd kick him out. He'd come back and I'd kick him out again. Finally, he realized I was serious.

Shortly after he moved, I found out I was pregnant. Tasha was born when I was seventeen. That was awful. There I was, seventeen years old with a kid and no job, living on welfare. The welfare gave me a hundred and twenty-eight dollars a month for me and Tasha. My rent was a hundred and ten. The utilities brought that to a hundred and fifteen. Ten dollars went for food stamps, and that left three dollars for whatever else we needed. I didn't have enough money for soap or to take the bus to the food stamp office, nothing! Once in a while my mom would give me a little money, but she had five kids to support, so she couldn't give me much.

Then, to make it even worse, the people from welfare would come around and check the house to make sure there weren't any guys living here. They'd come around every six months and you'd have to have all your utility bills and your rent receipts ready to show them.

When I was on welfare I wanted to get a job. I hated hanging around the house all day, but I had been shut in so long I was just like a turtle. My sister-in-law lived next door and I used to go over to her house every day, and we didn't have nothing to talk about— just the soap operas. We kept on telling each other we were going to get jobs, but we were both so scared. All she'd ever done was cook and clean house, and I'd just had a couple of part-time waitress jobs. But, finally, one day, we did it. We went down to the unemployment place and we both got jobs working at Lenkhurt. It's an electronics factory, and I work on components. I wind bobbins.

When I got the job at Lenkhurt, it was a real switch. Suddenly I was doing everything, raising a child, working, and taking care of the house. I was doing everything that a man and a woman do when they're in couples, and it felt real good because I didn't have to ask anybody for anything. Then, I started getting to know some of the men at work. Two of them bought me this old car, and now they're teaching me how to fix it up. Things started to change for me. I began to view men differently, and sometimes they saw me differently, too. Before, I'd sort of looked up at them, and now I started to look at them as equals.

The job I've got is a good job, too, considering that I dropped

out of high school and I've never had a full-time job before. There
are about fifteen hundred people working here. Most of the workers are women and most of the women are Chicanas like me,
without much education and with one or two kids to support.
You start out making two seventy-six, and then it goes up slowly
to three forty-five an hour. The only way you can make more
money than that is by incentive or piecework. That's when they
give you orders to do, like if you're supposed to do one hundred
pieces in an hour and you do two hundred, you get an extra hour's
pay. Some of the women here work two hundred percent—that
means in eight hours they get sixteen hours' worth of pieces
done, and they stick at it. I can't do that. Sometimes I can, but
not all the time. It gets to you.

We come into work at seven A.M. and we get off at five. We get
a break at nine A.M. for ten minutes, and then we get a half-hour
for lunch and a break in the afternoon. But from when you get
here, it's rush, rush, rush. And you have to punch in and punch
out. They have very strict rules. If you're tardy, they mark it
down, kinda like they do in high school. They mark down your
absences, too. You're only allowed to have a certain amount of
unexcused absences. Then you have to bring in a slip from the
doctor. They give you warnings and then they discipline you if
you miss too much. There's a lot of women here who have lost
their jobs for being late in the mornings. Like say they have kids,
and the nursery didn't open in time, or something like that.
That's not considered. A certain amount of absences or
tardies, and you're out.

We've got a union here now. It's been here for about a year, and
it's helped a little bit. We get thirty cents more an hour. From
what some of the women say, it's made things worse, though,
because before the union, they didn't have such a strict attendance policy. But I think that the company brings these policies
in on purpose so that people will think the union's not good for
you.

I'm a union steward. I volunteered about a year ago. When the
workers have complaints, I go talk to them and I try to settle it
with the supervisor, if possible. I also file grievances and things.

There's not very many women in the union. It's mostly men,
and I think the women are beginning to see that because they say,

"How come those men run the union when we're the ones that work here?" That's why I wanted to be a steward, so we'd have some representation, and the union caucus thought I should try it, too. They made me a steward, but they never gave me any training. If they wanted me so bad, they could have given me some training and prepared me. They have steward meetings, but the meetings only last a half an hour. Everybody just gets together and talks. There's a group of us now that are going to start training ourselves, since the union's not doing it, because we really could do a lot more if we were prepared.

About a year ago some of the guys in the union told me about this Chicano political group they belonged to, and invited me to come to some meetings. The men and women in that group tried really hard to treat each other as equals—even though the men failed a lot, they tried really hard. The women pointed out the way men were ignoring issues like child care. The men really listened. They started taking care of the kids during the meetings. This one couple in the group was invited to go to China, but she got pregnant so he had to go alone. After he got back, though, he got the other end of the deal. She's a photographer and she started working on this book, *450 Years of Chiciano Oppression*. So her husband stayed home and took care of the baby while she did the photography.

Most of the men I know are trying to understand the problems between men and women. I've got this one friend, he's a Black guy, his name is Alfred Jones. He's nineteen years old, and he's in prison up in Santa Fe. I go up to see him every Saturday, and we talk a lot about equality and the woman question. He's really new to the idea, but he's trying to learn, and he's talking to the other guys in the joint, and asking me for books to read about politics and about women. It makes me really happy to have friends like that.

There's a lot of men, though, who still don't see things my way. Like I'll go out with my friends to dances, and the men will get shocked at the way I act. They say, "Is it all right if I sit with you?" after I've danced with them, and if I tell them no, they're surprised and mad, but if I say yes, they think I like them. So they start holding my hand. I say, "What are you holding my hand for? I'm not a little kid." And they get really burned up and leave. So sometimes it's very hard.

I get along real good with the women at work, though. I can talk to them about more things than the men can, like about the kids and nurseries. When they put in that attendance policy, the women were mad. They said, "Well, if they're going to mark us down when we can't find day care for our kids, we're just going to leave our kids out by the entrance gate. We'll leave them in the guard shack and let the guards deal with them." And so I got to talking to the women about the nurseries they have in China, and how neat it would be to have something like that here. You could go have lunch with your kids, and you could go over to nurse them. So we've got this new demand for our next contract—we want a day-care center at the plant. We may not get it, but we're going to try, because day care is really important to us. And one of these days or years we will get it. I know we will.

# Glossary

*Abuelita.* Term of endearment for grandmother.

*Adobe.* Bricks made of mud and straw and dried in the sun, used in the construction of homes; a type of architecture native to the Southwest.

*Amole.* Yucca root, which is shaved and boiled; used primarily as a shampoo and as a soap for washing wool and linen.

*Barrio.* Urban Hispanic neighborhood, usually working-class.

*Bendición.* A blessing.

*Biscochitos.* Anise flavored sugar cookies, traditionally served at Christmas.

*Carajas.* Lazy ones; scoundrels; good-for-nothings.

*Chicanismo.* Chicano pride, a philosophy valuing those aspects of culture and life-style which are Chicano.

*Chiles.* Peppers, usually Anaheims, picked green, roasted and peeled, or left to turn red and then dried; the basis of many New Mexican dishes.

*Chimajá.* Indian parsley, boiled and drunk as a tea for weak and gassy stomach.

*Comadres.* (1) Relationship between a mother and the woman who baptizes her child; (2) relationship between mothers-in-law.

*Empanada, empanadita.* A pie or tart filled with fruit or with meat and spices; traditionally served at Christmas.

*Enchiladas.* Tortillas, usually rolled, spread with cheese, meat and/or beans and covered with red or green chile; in New Mexico, they are layered rather than rolled.

*Fiesta.* Holiday; community celebration.

*Frijoles.* Pinto beans; a staple of New Mexican cooking.

*Gringo.* Anglo; often, but not always, a pejorative term.

*Hermana.* Sister.

*¡Híjo! ¡Híjole!* An exclamation of surprise, exasperation, pain, or disbelief.

*Hipazote.* Leaf of the American wormseed plant.

*Huapango.* A song, usually of sadness or lament, in ⅜ time; emotional.

*La Marcha.* A traditional dance at a wedding, involving all participants; usually begins the wedding party.

*Macho.* Manliness; characteristics traditionally encouraged in males, such as strength, courage; an attitude of superiority; also used negatively, to refer to attitudes and behavior that demean women.

*Mariachi.* A type of music originating in the state of Jalisco, Mexico, but now popular throughout Mexico and the Southwest.

*Matanza.* Butchering; often a social event involving the slaughter, butchering, roasting, and feasting.

*Mi'hijita, mi'jita.* Term of endearment for a young woman; my daughter.

*Oshá.* (New Mexican pronunciation, *ocha.*) Porter's lovage; probably the single most used plant medicine in New Mexico, given for virtually every complaint, but especially to break up phlegm and to cure bronchial colds; the root is used as a disinfectant and skin wash, also boiled as a tea to induce sweating.

*Patrón.* Landlord; boss; often used to designate those who control and exploit Hispanic people.

*Posole.* Stew made with hominy, red chile, and pork or tripe; traditionally served at Christmas.

*Ranchera.* A song similar in style and function to country and western music; runs the gamut from sad ballad to happy love song.

*Raza.* People of Hispanic origin.

*Redondo.* Song sung in rounds, such as "Row, Row, Row Your Boat."

*Son.* A story set to song; the music is double-time.

*Sopa.* Common Spanish word for soup; in New Mexico, *sopa* is the term for a bread pudding made from cubes of toasted white bread, grated cheese, raisins, cinnamon, and a syrup derived from unrefined brown sugar; traditionally served at Christmas and Easter, the dish is also called *capirotada.*

*Tamale.* Red chile and pork in a corn-flour dough, wrapped in a corn husk and steamed.

*Tiempo.* Time; a euphemism for the menstrual period.

*Tortilla.* A flat, round bread made of flour or corn meal; used as an accompaniment to foods.

*Viejita.* Term of endearment for an elderly woman.

# About the Authors

NAN ELSASSER took her bachelor's degree in educational linguistics and her M.A. in secondary education at the University of New Mexico, Albuquerque. She has taught bilingual education courses at the University of New Mexico and at the University of Albuquerque, has held a Fulbright Teaching Fellowship at the College of the Bahamas, Nassau, and has taught female prison inmates basic reading and writing skills. Currently, she is developing curriculum for para-professionals and parents in the Head Start program, Albuquerque. She has published a number of articles on language and ethnicity.

KYLE MACKENZIE earned her B.A. in sociology at Skidmore College and her master's degree in elementary education at the University of Miami, Coral Gables. She has been an English teacher in private schools in Albuquerque and at the Academia La Castellana, Caracas, Venezuela. With Yvonne Tixier y Vigil and Nan Elsasser, she has published articles on New Mexican Hispanas, and is completing a book on literary New Mexico, 1925–1945. At present she is a doctoral candidate in the Department of American Studies, University of New Mexico, studying under a Danforth Graduate Fellowship.

YVONNE TIXIER Y VIGIL is an assistant professor of education at the University of Nebraska, Omaha. She took her B.A. in sociology and her M.A. in secondary education at the University of Albuquerque, receiving her Ph.D. in education from the University of Oklahoma. A reading specialist, she has a particular interest in the development of multicultural and bilingual reading materials. She has published articles on the learning process and on related subjects in educational and sociological journals.

# About the Photographer

SUSAN TROWBRIDGE is the design and production director of the *Women's Lives / Women's Work* project. She received a bachelor's degree in design and photography from the University of Michigan, Ann Arbor, and has worked as art director, graphic designer, and photographer for numerous publishers, including The Feminist Press. She has taught design, production, and publishing courses at the State University of New York. For the last fourteen years she has operated a free-lance design and consulting business, and is currently completing the M.B.A. program at New York University. She serves on the New York board of the Women's National Book Association and on the board of Free Life Editions.

# Index

Page numbers in *italics* refer to the captions of photographs.

# A Note on Language

In editing books, The Feminist Press attempts to eliminate harmful sex and race bias inherent in the language. In order to retain the authenticity of historical and literary documents, however, our policy is to leave their original language unaltered. We recognize that the task of changing language usage is extremely complex and that it will not be easily accomplished. The process is an ongoing one that we share with many others concerned with the relationship between a humane language and a more humane world.

---

*This book was composed on the VIP in Trump and Antique Olive by Monotype Composition Company, Baltimore, Maryland. It was printed and bound by R. R. Donnelley & Sons Company, Chicago, Illinois. The covers were printed by Algen Press, Queens, New York.*